Advance Praise for

HOW TO SURVIVE YOUR MARRI

"Full of honest advice from newlyweds and longtime couples.
This book answers the question–'How do other people do it?'"
—ELLEN SABIN, MPH, MPA
  EXECUTIVE DIRECTOR, "THE EQUALITY IN MARRIAGE INSTITUTE"

"A unique offering, and sorely needed resource, of advice/wisdom
from men and women who have found creative solutions to the many
challenges of marriage and now are reaping its rewards."
—MARCIA NADEL, JD, MFT (MARRIAGE FAMILY THERAPIST)

"How to Survive Your Marriage is a fun companion to research-based
marriage manuals. Great for starting a discussion with your partner
or laughing at the commonality of concerns that engaged couples
often face."
—DRS. PATRICK AND MICHELLE GANNON
  PSYCHOLOGISTS/COUPLES EXPERTS AND FOUNDERS OF MARRIAGE PREP 101
  WWW.MARRIAGEPREP101.COM

Praise for other HUNDREDS OF HEADS™ *guides:*

HOW TO SURVIVE YOUR FRESHMAN YEAR

"An amazing collection of tips, stories and fun. A *tour de force.*
A great send-off for every high school senior."
—JEFFREY P. KAHN, PH.D
  PROFESSOR, UNIVERSITY OF MINNESOTA, DIRECTOR, CENTER FOR BIOETHICS

"If only there had been a guide like this when I went to college,
I could have avoided a lot of mistakes."
—LESLIE GILBERT-LURIE
  PRESIDENT, LOS ANGELES COUNTY BOARD OF EDUCATION

HOW TO SURVIVE YOUR BABY'S FIRST YEAR

"An amazing kaleidoscope of insights into surviving parenthood, this book will reassure moms and dads that they are not alone in the often scary world of bringing up baby."

—JOSEF SOLOWAY, M.D., F.A.A.P.
CLINICAL ASSOCIATE PROFESSOR OF PEDIATRICS
WEILL MEDICAL COLLEGE OF CORNELL UNIVERSITY

"What to read when you're reading the other baby books. The perfect companion for your first-year baby experience."

—SUSAN REINGOLD, M.A.
EDUCATOR

"Full of real-life ideas and tips. If you love superb resource books for being the best parent you can be, you'll love *How to Survive Your Baby's First Year.*"

—ERIN BROWN CONROY, M.A.
MOTHER OF TWELVE, AUTHOR, COLUMNIST, AND CREATOR OF TOTALLYFITMOM.COM

HOW TO SURVIVE DATING

"I'm not a fan of the so-called experts. What do they know? This is the first book (and series) that gives it to you straight, from real people who have been there in the trenches. Unlike so many other self-help books, I actually read this one."

—STEVE LINOWES
WASHINGTON, DC

"A great handbook to one of life's best adventures. Hundreds of Heads sharing their wisdom. Practical, readable and fun."

—J.R. WILLIAMSON
ATLANTA, GEORGIA

"I couldn't put it down. The stories and advice are hilarious and wise. I can't wait to try some of this in the real world."

—LESLIE KIMERLING
NEW YORK, NEW YORK

How to
Survive
Your
Marriage

WARNING:

This Guide contains differing opinions. Hundreds of Heads will not always agree. Advice taken in combination may cause unwanted side effects. Use your Head when selecting advice.

How to · Survive Your Marriage

by Hundreds of Happy Couples Who Did *

*and some things to avoid, from a few ex-spouses who didn't™

edited by
YADIN KAUFMANN AND LORI BANOV KAUFMANN
with JAMIE ALLEN

Hundreds of Heads Books, Inc.
ATLANTA

Illustrations © 2004 by Image Club
See page 255 for credits and permissions.

Library of Congress Cataloging-in-Publication Data.
How to survive your marriage / by hundreds of happy couples who did, and some things to avoid from a few ex-spouses who didn't; edited by Yadin Kaufmann and Lori Banov Kaufmann with Jamie Allen.
    p. cm. -- (Hundreds of heads survival guide)
  ISBN 0-9746292-4-3
  1. Marriage. I. Kaufmann, Yadin. II. Kaufmann, Lori Banov. III.
Allen, Jamie, 1968- IV. Series.
  HQ734.H8655 2005
  646.7'8--dc22

2004027879

Cover and book design by Elizabeth Johnsboen

Cover photograph by PictureQuest
Interior illustrations by Image Club

HUNDREDS OF HEADS™ books are available at special discounts when purchased in bulk for premiums or institutional or educational use. Excerpts and custom editions can be created for specific uses. For more information, please email sales@hundredsofheads.com or write to:

HUNDREDS OF HEADS BOOKS, INC.
#230
2221 Peachtree Road, Suite D
Atlanta, GA 30309

ISBN 0-9746292-4-3

Printed in U.S.A.
10 9 8 7 6 5 4 3 2 1

CONTENTS

Introduction

Whether you are just about to take the big plunge or have already been married for 50 years, you probably realize just what a huge challenge marriage can be. Take two completely separate people, with different sets of experiences and differing sizes of "luggage," walk them down the aisle, and then watch them try to meld those two lives into one. The result can be anything from wedded bliss to horror story.

This book, the fourth in the HUNDREDS OF HEADS Survival Guide series, grew out of the simple idea that when you're facing any of life's major challenges—like deciding whether to say two simple words like "I do" or rather to head for the hills—it's good to get advice from people who have "been there, done that." Getting married and surviving your relationship with your beloved partner is hard work—why try to navigate these waters yourself?

Other advice books, no matter how smart or expert their authors, are generally limited to the knowledge of only one or two people. This book takes a different approach: our "headhunters" have talked to hundreds of people about their marriage experiences, and compiled the best advice here for your benefit. If two heads are better than one, as the saying goes, then we think hundreds of them are even better.

As you read through this book, you'll see that we all struggle with the same questions: How do men and women communicate? Should we have separate or joint checking accounts? Why does he always leave the seat up, and why does she care? Why are the in-laws so hard to deal with? Who takes out the trash and who does the laundry? How do you make time for romance in your hectic life? You'll also gain the invaluable knowledge gleaned from people all over the country, of various ages and marital experience, who have developed their own strategies for long-term compatibility.

Of course, with so many interviewees, we often found people with starkly opposite views on the same issues. For your benefit, we've put them all together, so that you'll sometimes see two very different pieces of advice right next to one another. It's up to you to decide which approach works for you and your spouse. You may not agree with a particular respondent's point of view, but in this book you can choose from hundreds of others.

So read on. With so many stories to read and so much to learn, you can't lose. Being married is one of the most difficult things you can do: It will test the limits of your compassion, your ability to compromise and communicate, your parenting style, your very sense of self. But, of course, marriage is also one of life's most rewarding journeys. Our advice: Don't go it alone.

Yadin Kaufmann

Lori Banov Kaufmann

LITTLE HEADS

So you'll know just how expert our respondents really are, we've included their credentials in this book. Look for these icons:

      = Married   ʏ = Years

      = Engaged   ᴍ = Months

      = Divorced

This Is It: Getting Engaged and Planning the Wedding

C ontrary to popular belief, married life doesn't begin when you actually get married. It begins the moment you or your spouse answers, "Yeah, sure" to the popped question: "Will you marry me?" From that moment on, riding a wave of love and congratulations, you are thrown into one of the most demanding times of your new life together: planning a wedding. From pulling off a clever engagement, to staying afloat in a sea of gift registries, flower arrangements and future in-laws, here are your survival tricks of the trade.

MY FIANCÉ TOOK A DAY OFF OF WORK to drive from Chicago to Iowa and ask my parents for my hand in marriage. They were really touched by it.

—*ANN MAGNER*
CHICAGO, ILLINOIS
5M

DO NOT LET YOUR FAMILY RUN YOUR WEDDING.

—*ALLISON BENOIT*
HOUMA, LOUSIANA
1M

POP THE QUESTION ON VACATION. Once arriving at our condo in Kauai, I quickly moved her out of the room and onto the beach. It was raining, but my excuse was that I didn't fly 8 hours to not see the beach. It was Valentine's Day 2003 and I walked her over to a rock and asked her to close her eyes while I wrote a love poem in the sand as her gift. I cleared off the sand and wrote, "Will You Marry Me?" Then, I walked her back in front of me and she slowly opened her eyes to these words and me kneeling behind with her ring.

—*M.T.*
SEATTLE, WASHINGTON
2M

• • • • • • • • •

DON'T PROPOSE ON A HOLIDAY. The proposal needs to be special on its own. My husband waited until the weekend after my birthday to propose, which was great because I didn't suspect anything. When he took me on a gondola ride in Newport Beach, I figured we were still celebrating. Instead, as we floated down the water, our guide asked me to pick up a glass bottle that was floating outside our boat. Inside, was a proposal note from my husband.

—*S.A.*
LAKE FOREST, CALIFORNIA
6Y

• • • • • • • • •

YOU GET ENGAGED ONCE, so do something special. I shocked my girlfriend by proposing the night we had to go pick my sister up from the airport. When we parked the car I got out a couple bags I'd packed and surprised her even more by taking her to Los Angeles and then on a cruise for a long weekend.

—*JOE SCHWAB*
DENVER, COLORADO
1M

I proposed to my husband. I didn't get down on one knee. We weren't in a position to do that.

—*DEB S.*
SAN DIEGO, CALIFORNIA
27Y

MY THEN-FIANCÉ BOUGHT ME THE RING of my choice and promised to love me forever. I was thrilled! However, I just couldn't give up the whole shopping experience. I later found a ring I liked better. I called my fiancé from the mall and asked if I could exchange the rings. He said, "Well, how much does it cost?" I said, "Less than the original." He said, "NOW THAT'S THE KIND OF GIRL I WANT TO MARRY!"

—*TARY PARIS*
LINCOLN, NEBRASKA
10Y

· · · · · · · ·

Planning a wedding is a good time to practice that whole compromise thing.

—*LIZ WASHBURN*
COLUMBIA, MISSOURI

· · · · · · · ·

AFTER WE ANNOUNCED OUR ENGAGEMENT, my family started giving us all their ideas about a big traditional wedding. I wanted to keep everything simple but was letting my family talk me out of my plans. Finally, my husband reminded me that it was me getting married and not my family, and we went ahead with our plans of getting married, just the two of us. No matter how excited your family gets, don't ever lose track of what the bride and groom want. You're the two that matter.

—*ALLISON BENOIT*
HOUMA, LOUISIANA
1M

PAY ATTENTION TO WHAT YOUR GIRLFRIEND talks about, because you can get really creative proposal ideas this way. My girlfriend had been hounding me for weeks about this 32" TV she wanted, so for Christmas, I got this huge box and wrapped it up to look like the TV. Inside, however, were about seven smaller boxes that fit inside one another. The last box she unwrapped was the smallest one—and inside, was her ring.

—*ANONYMOUS*
CASTLE ROCK, COLORADO
5Y

. . . .

" To save money, we chose a Sunday when few weddings are scheduled, so we got a pretty good deal on the venue. "

—*R.J.*
REDMOND, WASHINGTON
10Y

. . . .

BUY BLANK VIDEOTAPES FOR THE PERSON taping your wedding. My husband's friend videotaped our wedding. Without previewing the tape, I took it to work to show my coworkers. During our lunch hour, we viewed the tape in a conference room. The tape was only 20 minutes long and when it ended it switched to a porno. It was the most embarrassing moment of my life. My friends teased me about wanting to see the wedding and not the honeymoon. It was awful. Then, the guy had the nerve to ask for the tape back.

—*D.L.*
CHICAGO, ILLINOIS
6Y

SHE HAD ALREADY PICKED OUT the engagement ring. We both went to pick it up. So, I go in, pay for it and bring it back to the car. She was very excited about getting the ring. I took her hand, looked in her eyes and said, "Will you marry me?" She said, "Yeah, yeah, yeah, give me my ring." I remind her of that sometimes.

> —*K. BECKERING*
> *SYRACUSE, NEW YORK*
> 8Y

. . . .

COMBINE A FAVORITE HOBBY with the proposal. I love to read. So my husband bought me a beautiful hardcover book of poetry. He glued the second half of the book's pages together, and then he hollowed out a space inside the book for the ring and marked that spot with a ribbon bookmark! Then he built a special box out of sturdy cardboard that fit the book exactly, and he covered the box with beautiful black velvet fabric, decorated with a burgundy velvet bow. I was so completely shocked when I opened that box! It was such a special time and such a creative proposal. We keep the beautiful velvet box in the china cabinet in our dining room. I just love it!

> —*JENNIFER BRIGHT REICH*
> *HELLERTOWN, PENNSYLVANIA*
> 1Y

. . . .

INVOLVE YOUR FIANCÉ IN THE LITTLE decisions to make him feel like he's helping. For example, I let him choose between yellow or periwinkle bridesmaids dresses. I knew he'd pick yellow, which was my number one choice, but it made him feel good to be able to pick things I cared about.

> —*A.D.*
> *MINNEAPOLIS, MINNESOTA*
> 10M

Guys, you always hear, "It's her wedding." It's true. Even if she says, "No, it's our wedding," it's really hers.

> —*SAM C.*
> *INDIANAPOLIS, INDIANA*

SURPRISE PROPOSALS AREN'T NECESSARILY a good thing. I'd planned on asking my wife to marry me during a romantic hike. However, because she had no idea what was coming, she insisted we bring our dog. Unfortunately, dogs can't do the hike I wanted to do, so I was forced to find another trail. It turned out to be a memorial to a bunch of firefighters who had died while battling a blaze. When we got to the top, we were surrounded by graves, which was hardly romantic. We were also so exhausted that I decided not to propose until we got back to the hotel. In hindsight, I wish I would've given my wife some sort of clue about what was coming that day.

—*RANDY FREITIK*
PEORIA, ILLINOIS
8Y

SPOTLIGHT THIS ENGAGEMENT

THE PROPOSAL IS ABOUT DOING SOMETHING COMPLETELY UNIQUE because she's the most special person to you. For our proposal, I told my wife that I had to interview a band at the Fox Theater in Atlanta. I've taken her to interviews before, so she was not surprised. We arrived at the back of the theater (as I had arranged), and the theater director dismissed himself as he led us through to the stage. There we were, on the stage of one of the most beautiful theaters in the world. Then the orchestra started playing our song, and my wife was really in shock. She dropped her purse in the orchestra pit. The spotlight shined on me as I turned to her with the ring. She was so floored, I had to hold her up. She accepted, and we danced under the theater's blue sky to the music I had chosen for us.

—*JOSHUA LEVS*
ATLANTA, GA
4Y

IF YOUR MOM CAN'T HELP YOU with your wedding, get creative. My mother would normally have played a big role in planning my wedding but since she wasn't in town, our preacher's wife did some of the things she would have. She was kind of like a drill sergeant, making sure everyone was in their place and that the big picture was on target. And she came with the preacher for the same fee!

—ANONYMOUS
SAN ANTONIO, TEXAS
5Y

> **Once you get engaged, a world of wedding hell is thrust upon you. If you think planning a wedding is fun, you probably aren't the one getting married. Eloping to Vegas never sounded so good.**
>
> —MITCH S.
> CHICAGO, ILLINOIS
> 5M

DON'T SET A WEDDING DATE that will be during deer season. If it has to be in the fall, during hunting time, pick bird season—that way you'll only piss off one or two of your friends.

—RUTH CORNETT
LANSING, MICHIGAN
4Y

USE VISUAL AIDS. I was managing most of the wedding details, trying to keep him involved by asking for his opinions. More often than not his reply was "I don't care." You can imagine my surprise when after a few weeks, he complained that he wasn't involved enough in the planning of our wedding! Desperate for a way to help him to get involved, I took huge pieces of poster board and cut pictures of items from wedding magazines and made an idea map. This helped us to make critical decisions such as what types of rings we wanted, what types of food to serve at the reception, and more. I still use this technique from time to time when I'm stuck with a problem.

—CAROL GILMORE
EASTON, PENNSYLVANIA
💕13Y

. . . .

SPEND MONEY ON YOUR PHOTOGRAPHER. We tried to cut costs there and it was a nightmare. Not only did he take eight months to return our photos, but many of them were messed up and dirty when we finally got them back. Seriously, you can save money on flowers and centerpieces (which die anyway) and party favors, which people forget to bring home. But wedding pictures last forever.

—WREN JOHNSON
CENTENNIAL, COLORADO
💕1Y

. . . .

LADIES, DON'T TORTURE YOUR FUTURE HUSBAND with the task of gift registries. Go with your mom, go with a friend. Go with anybody except the man you are going to marry. I did not bring mine and it was perfect. I know friends who did . . . NIGHTMARE!

—L.S.
SHARON, MASSACHUSETTS
💕8Y

A new trend for engaged couples is to declare sack sessions off-limits in the weeks before the wedding. Banning bedroom play guarantees that honeymoon sex will be as hot as possible.

—COSMOPOLITAN
MAGAZINE

IF I COULD HAVE DONE ANYTHING DIFFERENTLY, I would have started saving money for a wedding years before so I could have had the type of party I wanted to have afterward.

—*MONICA Y. DENNIS*
BRIDGEPORT, CONNECTICUT
3Y

• • • • • • • •

HIRE SOMEONE TO PLAN THE WEDDING. We fought a lot, and the moms made it so hard. If I did it over again, I'd just hire someone.

—*CHELI BROWN*
ATLANTA, GEORGIA
1Y

• • • • • • • •

I KNOW FROM PERSONAL EXPERIENCE that you can plan an amazing wedding in three weeks. I did it. All you have to do is make sure you don't get attached to any single detail. I wasn't married to any particular kind of flower. I didn't have a specific type of dress I had to have. And it all came through perfectly. I concentrated on making sure it was good enough. And everyone tells me it was the best wedding they'd ever been to.

—*HANIA*
SEATTLE, WASHINGTON
1Y

• • • • • • • •

DO NOT ASK YOUR HUSBAND TO PARTICIPATE in the gift registry unless he has a keen interest in it. You will end up with strange-looking china, stranger-looking silverware and bizarre glassware. It is best to leave this to those who care for it. My husband couldn't pick our dishes out of a line-up, even though he uses them everyday.

—*ANONYMOUS*
SINGER ISLAND, FLORIDA
7Y

Have an open bar. I can't stress this enough. If you want to have a fun wedding, have an open bar.

—*DAN TWETTEN*
CHICAGO, ILLINOIS
4Y

PRENUP, THUMBS UP?

I'VE BEEN A DIVORCE ATTORNEY for 28 years. I recommend that everyone get a prenuptial agreement. This way, you specify exactly what happens to your finances during your marriage, and you also know what will happen if the marriage ends. If you don't have an agreement and your marriage ends, you go to the courts and are dependent upon the subjective opinions of the judge. You have no certainty what will happen then. I have to admit my wife and I didn't have a prenup when we were married 28 years ago. But if I had it to do over again, I would get one. I think that she would, too.

> —BOB NACHSHIN
> LOS ANGELES, CALIFORNIA
> 28Y

IT WASN'T A LEGAL DOCUMENT, but we laughingly say our prenuptial agreement was, "No pets, no kids, no lawn." We knew going into our marriage that we didn't want to have children—we felt it was too late for us to get started on family and our relationship would be better without children. I love animals but I'm allergic to almost all of them and my husband didn't grow up with pets in his household, so we knew we didn't want to have pets. It's also something else to take care of. It's kind of liberating not to have to walk the dog at night. We're not interested in having a showplace of a house; even mowing the lawn would be a waste of energy that we'd rather spend on something else more valuable to us. Some might say that we're horribly self-absorbed, but it works for us.

> —J.H.
> ATHENS, GEORGIA
> 5Y

PRENUPTIAL AGREEMENTS? Oh, hell no. We decided to marry, bad credit and all.

> —SARAH CLARK
> NEW YORK, NEW YORK
> 2Y

YOU DON'T MARRY SOMEONE FOR THEIR THINGS. You marry them for their heart. We didn't have anything we wouldn't want to share with the other or try to take from the other, no matter how much it was worth.

—*NIQUIE RAGLAND*
NASHVILLE, TENNESSEE
3Y

• • • • • • • •

PRENUPS ARE USEFUL FOR MANY people—especially for people who marry and who already have families who might be concerned about their inheritance. They are also attractive in cases where there's a huge disparity in net worth between husband and wife, so that in the case of separation or divorce, they can return to the relative financial status they had before the marriage.

—*L.B.*
CINCINNATI, OHIO
35Y

• • • • • • • •

HONESTLY, I FEEL THAT IF ANYONE IS WORRIED enough about their assets to sign a prenup, then they are not selfless enough or trusting enough to handle a marriage. The union of marriage includes everything, even material things.

—*WHITNEY JASINSKI*
RENTON, WASHINGTON
3Y

• • • • • • • •

WE DID NOT SIGN A PRENUPTIAL AGREEMENT; it was never an issue. From day one of our relationship, we have shared everything with one another and don't distinguish between who has what. Love is about sharing and becoming partners and bringing everything you have to the table.

—*CATHY RINGER*
EVERETT, MASSACHUSETTS
LESS THAN 1Y

AT THE BEGINNING OF THE PLANNING PROCESS, establish who will pay for what. My sisters-in-law, for example, assumed we would fly the two of them plus their entire families across the country to the wedding on our dollar. They also assumed we would be paying for their lodging bills once they got here. This was not the case. We were willing to fly my husband's elderly mother, but somewhere along the line, my husband's sisters assumed we would be including them in our largesse.

—HELEN COVINGTON
DURHAM, NORTH CAROLINA
8Y

• • • • • • • •

"You do?
I do, too!"
In early
American
Colonial times,
a man and
woman were
considered
married if
they simply
said they
were.
—SEATTLE TIMES

NOW THAT I'VE BEEN MARRIED FOR A YEAR, my husband and I have begun to give cash as a wedding gift. Half the stuff I registered for has not been used yet—you get a little over-zealous when you're walking around Crate & Barrel or Williams-Sonoma with your "stun gun," zapping all the items you want. Not to write off the combination juicer/pasta maker (I believe it has different ports for each function), but 15 months later, it's still in a box in the garage.

—JANE M.
CORTE MADERA, CALIFORNIA
1Y

• • • • • • • •

ON GIFT REGISTRIES . . . Someone told me (and for some reason I listened) that you want to be prepared to have Thanksgiving dinner in your house. I'm still waiting for the day—I've never cooked a turkey in my life, but if I ever do, we'll all have place settings.

—ANONYMOUS
NEW YORK, NEW YORK
2Y

STAND YOUR GROUND. Planning a wedding can be very stressful—especially when others are involved. I fought with my stepmother about my bridesmaids' dresses. I chose different patterns and styles—all the same colors, but different cuts because people have different body types. I was trying to do what would look nice for each bridesmaid. She said, "You can't do that." I said, "Yes, I can. It's my wedding."

—*M.B.*
SYRACUSE, NEW YORK
8Y

• • • • • • • •

Passing on prenuptials: Only 5-10% of marrying Americans get prenuptial agreements.

—*HARVARD UNIVERSITY GAZETTE*

AS MUCH AS OLD-FASHIONED RELATIVES look down on "living in sin," it helps to live with your fiancé before you get married. It teaches you what type of person you'll be living with for the rest of your life.

—*SUSAN MAROSITZ*
CLIFTON, NEW JERSEY
4Y

• • • • • • • •

WHAT'S IN A NAME?

I KEPT MY MAIDEN NAME. I felt that using my first name and my husband's last name was like having a made-up identity.

—*D.P.*
SANTA CLARA, CALIFORNIA
2Y

• • • • • • • •

I WOULD JOKE WITH PEOPLE if they asked me if I was taking my husband's name. I'd say, "Yes, I actually plan to take both his first name and his last name."

—*ANONYMOUS*
LOS ANGELES, CALIFORNIA
3Y

In China, nearly 20 million people get married every year, but first they have to pass the pre-marital medical examination.

—*WWW.BMJ.COM*

WE CALLED OFF OUR ENGAGEMENT at one point because we fought so much during the wedding planning. We broke up for three months. And then we got back together and considered life-long cohabitation before getting married, just because the whole idea of planning a wedding was so daunting. But we ended up having a really casual, small wedding. We wanted a party where someone threw out vows in the middle, and that's exactly what we did.

—*TIM MURPHINE*
VALDOSTA, GEORGIA
♥4Y

• • • • • • • •

I WILL NEVER UNDERSTAND WHY ANYONE in the world would chose to marry someone these days without living with them first. Come on: this is 2004, not 1944! The reasons for living together prior to engagement are plentiful—seeing how you respond to each other with continuous contact, learning more about each other's personal habits, daily acts of consideration, levels of affection, etc. To me, if the woman I wanted to marry would not live with me before we got engaged, this would be a clear sign that we were not on the same wave-length.

J.S.B.
SYDNEY, AUSTRALIA
♥2M

• • • • • • • •

WE WROTE OUR OWN CEREMONY, with some help from our Unitarian minister. It was a great experience, and we learned more about what we wanted from our marriage in the process of writing our vows and choosing specific passages.

—*ANONYMOUS*
BOSTON, MASSACHUSETTS
♥2Y

The Big Day: Wedding Wisdom and Honeymoon Help

*Y*ou've spent months getting everything just right: dreaming about lavender bridesmaid dresses and china place settings, waking up in a cold sweat as the reality of "till death do us part" sinks in. You may be surprised to know that no matter how long weddings take to plan, they are over in a matter of hours. Here are some wise words about how to enjoy the happiest day of your life, and where to go to unwind when it's all over.

MY MOM SAID THE DAY I GOT MARRIED and started my own life was the happiest day of her life. When I thought about it later, I wasn't sure how to take that.

—*S. GUPTA*
FROSTBURG, MARYLAND
9M

IF I COULD DO ONE THING DIFFERENTLY ON MY WEDDING DAY, WHAT WOULD IT BE? ELOPE!

—*J.D.*
ATLANTA, GEORGIA
5Y

I STRONGLY ENCOURAGE PEOPLE to have the kind of wedding that they want to have. It's hard to resist family pressures, but after all it's your wedding, not theirs! My wife and I were both married before, each in traditional church weddings with about one hundred people in attendance. That hadn't worked out so well for either of us, so we decided to do something completely different the second time around. We started thinking about an inexpensive destination wedding and honeymoon for just the two of us because we only had a few thousands dollars saved for both the wedding and a down payment on our house. In the end, we chose a wonderful wedding/honeymoon combination at Walt Disney World in Florida. We were married at the happiest place on earth. What a great way to start our new life together!

—*MICHAEL REICH*
HELLERTOWN, PENNSYLVANIA
1Y

• • • • • • • • •

THE ONE THING I WISH WE HAD DONE at our wedding was create a professional video. Not so much as a memory for me and my husband, but because I think our daughter would have loved to see this event and the time before we were "Mommy and Daddy."

—*SUZANNE WILLIN*
WOODACRE, CALIFORNIA
5Y

More than 110,000 people marry in Las Vegas every year.

—TOP **10** OF EVERYTHING

• • • • • • • • •

WE ELOPED. We were both working and didn't have a lot of extra cash or vacation days. The benefit of eloping was that we were in control of our day. We didn't spend a lot of time or money on what ultimately is a fifteen minute ceremony. We spent money on our honeymoon instead!

—*JAN ALDER*
ATLANTA, GEORGIA
7Y

I KNOW THERE'S A TRADITION ABOUT not seeing the bride the day of the wedding, but we ignored that. About thirty minutes before the ceremony started, my husband came downstairs to the basement of the church so we could have a few quiet moments alone together. It was so special to have some private time before the rest of the day was spent with friends and family.

—*KELLY JAMES-ENGER*
DOWNERS GROVE, ILLINOIS
7Y

· · · · · · · ·

"The best part about my wedding was that moment right before the pastor said, 'You may kiss the bride' and my husband reached up and touched my face and it was like a 'soul kiss' for lack of a better phrase."

—*TONYA LEE*
MOUNT AIRY, MARYLAND
11Y

· · · · · · · ·

MY WEDDING WAS PERFECT. We had thirty people in a beautiful local inn. An expression of your love has nothing to do with spending $15,000 on a one-day party.

—*DAN*
HELOTES, TEXAS
3Y

AT YOUR WEDDING NO MORE THAN SIX PEOPLE
should be present. That's what we did, and it was
very easy and manageable. We see so many of
our friends getting stressed out trying to meet
other people's agendas. At our wedding, the only
guests were two justices and two witnesses. We
have no regrets about that day.

> —*J.P.*
> *HOBOKEN, NEW JERSEY*
> 9Y

. . . .

YOU HAVE TO MAKE YOUR WEDDING FUN. I think in
twenty-five years, I'm going to remember most
how fun our day was. We had great food, good
music, and dancing, and all of the people who
have loved and cared about us throughout our
lives were there to share it with us.

> —*KAREN G. STEWART*
> *PALM BEACH GARDENS, FLORIDA*
> 6M

. . . .

EVERYONE TOLD US WE HAD THE BEST reception.
Probably because we had an open bar and everyone partied until after midnight. If you watch the
video now, you'll see people doing very strange
dances. Also, one of my buddies did this "YMCA"
dance for the crowd. And another one of my
friends has this ability to do Mick Jagger perfectly.
So, there was plenty of entertainment.

> —*JWAIII*
> *ATLANTA, GEORGIA*
> 9Y

. . . .

WE BASICALLY ELOPED, and I would recommend it
highly. A month later we bought a house and had
a big party. But the pressure was off.

> —*J.L.E.*
> *PORTLAND, MAINE*
> 20Y

ON YOUR WEDDING DAY, don't decide that it would be relaxing to hit the outdoor hot-tub without sunscreen for 15 minutes on an overcast July day or you'll forever be immortalized as a tomato!

—*CHRISTINE BEIDEL*
RUTHERFORD, NEW JERSEY
3Y

● ● ● ● ● ● ● ●

KEEP THE WEDDING SIMPLE so you can have fun. When you have a big deal, people get so stressed. Try and relax and keep it within your financial means. We had a small wedding at my husband's uncle's house in New Hampshire, a lovely shingle-style house that overlooked fields and woods. I made all the food, including the wedding cake. My mother-in-law picked wild trillium and made my bouquet. I wore a vintage dress and my husband wore a Brooks Brothers suit. The justice of the peace said, "Do you want the short version or the long version?" and we both said, "The short version!" We enjoyed ourselves quite a bit—in fact, we enjoyed ourselves so much they had to make us leave our own wedding.

—*NAN HADDEN*
PORTLAND, MAINE
30Y

● ● ● ● ● ● ● ●

HAVE YOUR WEDDING OUT OF TOWN in a meaningful vacation-type setting. My wife and I live in San Antonio but we got married at my aunt's summer cottage in Cape May, New Jersey, where I had spent a lot of time growing up. Because we were away, a lot of people couldn't make it and as a result only very close relatives ended up coming. Both of our families got to know each other better as a result of the pared-down circumstance.

—*ANONYMOUS*
SAN ANTONIO, TEXAS
12Y

The largest underwater wedding took place on September 13, 2003. An estimated 105 divers (including the bride, groom and minister) submerged themselves in the waters of Rainbow Beach, St. Croix, for the marriage ceremony. (We're imagining the reception had a great buffet of crab legs.)

—*GUINNESS BOOK OF WORLD RECORDS*

WEDDING DRESS BLOOPERS

ALL WOMEN KNOW EXACTLY HOW UNCOMFORTABLE a strapless bra is, and how difficult it is to find one that meets your needs. After hours of shopping for the perfect bra, I decided to forego the foundation undergarment altogether. My dress didn't look different with or without a bra and it was snug enough to hold everything in place . . . or so I thought.

At the reception after the wedding, during a particularly long and energetic hora (traditional Jewish celebratory dance), the top of my dress slipped lower and lower until both breasts were covered only by the sheer illusion fabric that covered my dress. The good news is that my mother and new husband (oh, and the photographer) were the only ones to catch the situation. My new husband grabbed me and pulled me toward him, whispering in my ear "Your boobs are showing!" We clutched each other and shimmied off the dance floor into an adjacent room where I was able to "readjust my set" in private. The best part is the photo, which shows a perfect view of my "indecent exposure."

—*P.S.*
SAN FRANCISCO, CALIFORNIA
💔*1Y*

BUY YOUR DRESS FAR IN ADVANCE OF THE WEDDING. Although my dress was ready three weeks before the wedding, I had to get it altered. After I got it altered, I had to have it drycleaned. When I got it back from drycleaning, I took it out of the bag and it had a tear on the front. This was two days before the wedding. If I had allowed myself more time to find the dress, I probably wouldn't have run into all those problems.

—*ANDREA COX*
GRAND LAKE, COLORADO
💔*13Y*

• • • • • • • • •

MY HUSBAND AND I ENTERED A PERIOD of "forced abstinence"—what the Catholic Church calls "renewed virginity"—during the time leading up to our engagement party. Planning this big engagement party was somewhat stressful, so to let off a little steam, my fiancé and I had sex. I got pregnant. Six months later, I was married in a large flower-printed Hawaiian sheath—well, more like a muumuu. To make light of the situation, when my husband dug into his pocket to get the wedding ring, he pulled out a condom instead, exclaiming, "Oh, that's where it was!"

—*THERESA*
SAN FRANCISCO, CALIFORNIA
💔*4Y*

Why are there so many stories about "getting to the church on time?" Is it really that hard to do?

—C.S.
SAN FRANCISCO,
CALIFORNIA
4Y

DO NOT SCHEDULE THE WHOLE THING without putting aside any time for each other. We had family coming from out of town and spent the whole week entertaining. We didn't see each other alone until several days after the wedding reception, and then had a big blowup about the bachelor party, which occurred the night before the wedding (another no-no).

—A.T.
ARLINGTON, MASSACHUSETTS
13Y

. . . .

JUST ROLL WITH IT. Don't spend that night going, "Hey, I can't believe I don't have what I want here." I told people what I wanted in no uncertain terms and so many things went differently: the photographer was supposed to shoot half of the ceremony in black and white but he shot the whole thing in color, my hair stylist decided to do what she wanted to do with my hair instead of what I wanted, the caterer didn't put any fans out for our outdoor reception, even though we talked about it a gazillion times. These were all disappointments, especially since we'd spent so much money. But you know what? In the end, we were still married!

—J.B.H.
ALEXANDRIA, VIRGINIA
2Y

. . . .

MY HUSBAND AND I PUT FIVE DESTINATIONS in a hat and just picked one for our honeymoon so there were no hard feelings about who chose where we went. It ended up being Maui, Hawaii and it was one of the best weeks of my life.

—SARAH MICKEY
EVANSTON, ILLINOIS
4Y

DON'T LET YOURSELF BE A BRIDEZILLA on your wedding day. Stop all your last-minute preparations beginning at noon on the day before your wedding. Leave the work to others. From that moment on, relax and enjoy the next day and a half. Go to a spa, get your hair done, polish your nails. Accept that you've done your best and whatever else happens is out of your hands.

—*TEENA GOMEZ*
CORONA, CALIFORNIA
NEWLYWED

• • • • • • • • •

" Be a guest at your wedding. Don't get caught up in whether or not the head table is facing twenty-five degrees to the north/northwest of the band or if the flowers are the correct hue of magnolia blue. Nobody cares. Have fun! "

—*L.S.*
SHARON, MASSACHUSETTS
8Y

Eat your heart out, Elizabeth Taylor: A 72-year-old Malaysian man, who first tied the knot in 1957, has been married 53 times (so far). His latest wife: the one he married in 1957.

—*ASSOCIATED PRESS*

MAKE SURE YOU MEET MOST OF THE PEOPLE you're going to be shaking hands with before you get to the wedding. I had met most of my wife's immediate aunts and uncles and her cousins earlier, but the extended family I met at the wedding. At the end of the wedding, we were outside shaking everybody's hands and it was like, "Hi, nice to see you. Who are you?"

—*W.D.O.*
ATHENS, GEORGIA
4Y

• • • • • • • •

DON'T TRY TO MEMORIZE YOUR VOWS, even if you wrote them yourself and even if they're short! Have a piece of paper there to read off of. I had them so perfectly memorized I could have recited them in my sleep. But still, when I got up there and was actually getting married, my head was in such a daze, I just blanked completely. Luckily, my best man, who'd already been married himself, knew this would happen and had a copy of my vows in his pocket.

—*J.R.*
CHICAGO, ILLINOIS
5Y

• • • • • • • •

ENJOYING THE PROCESS IS MORE IMPORTANT than any single detail of your wedding. When I got married, there was supposed to be a trumpet player playing with the organist as I walked down the aisle. He didn't show up until an hour after he was supposed to. And the whole time I was walking down the aisle all I could think was, "Where is the trumpet player?" I lost out on that special moment of walking down the aisle because I was too stressed out about a detail that in the end didn't matter.

—*M.J.W.*
KIRKLAND, WASHINGTON
7Y

007 TIES THE KNOT

On our wedding day, we were surrounded by my parents and my sister and a few good friends on a sailboat off of Isla Mujeres, Mexico. Before the ceremony began, my husband-to-be accidentally ran the boat onto a reef after the boat's captain gave him the wheel (with little direction). So we had to have our ceremony on the well-grounded boat in the inlet instead of going out into the Gulf of Mexico to get married with the spectacular sunset in the background. Next, we all enjoyed cocktails and ceviche while the marina crew struggled to dislodge our boat. The boat wouldn't budge and it was now dark and cold, so we ended up being whisked to shore in a motorized dingy (which had to make several trips to transfer all 12 of us).

I remember feeling like a James Bond girl as I hung on tight to the railing of the dingy, my hair and wedding dress blowing wildly as I zipped across the black water into the night towards a remote dock in a foreign land. We all had to wait on a quiet, desolate road for a couple of Nissan Sentra taxicabs to come pick us up and take us back to town. The whole episode probably sounds a bit disastrous, but it was actually quite fun and adventurous. And now it's a big joke between my father and my husband when Dad advises Mike to "keep it in the channel."

—*SHANNON*
BOCA RATON, FLORIDA
2Y

DITCH THE GARTER TOSS. In my opinion, it's all about the objectification of women. At the reception, I couldn't stand the idea of it, so we didn't do it. Nobody even noticed that it was missing.

—COURTNEY ALFORD-POMEROY
ATHENS, GEORGIA
1Y

• • • • • • • •

" It's easy to pull off the perfect fairy-tale wedding. It's that 'happily ever after' that no one's figured out how to condense into magazine format yet. "

—ASHLEY O'DELL
NEW YORK, NEW YORK
10Y

• • • • • • • •

I WOULDN'T CHANGE A THING, EXCEPT that I wish I could have gotten more sleep the night before.

—ANONYMOUS
BOSTON, MASSACHUSETTS
2Y

• • • • • • • •

WE GOT MARRIED AT THE GRACELAND CHAPEL in Vegas with an Elvis impersonator as a witness.

—KAMMY T.
SAN FRANCISCO, CALIFORNIA
3Y

AT OUR WEDDING, WE DIDN'T do the bouquet toss. Instead, we did the anniversary dance. We had the band play my parents' wedding song and all the married couples went on the dance floor to dance, with the band having them step aside as they called out years of marriage. The last couple standing had been married for 52 years. The band leader asked them if they had any marriage advice for me and my husband. The husband said a few words about us having a "bella notte" and a "bella vita." Then his wife grabbed the mike and said, in her thickly accented English, "Marriage . . . It's not all a bed of roses, and then children arrive and all is forgiven."

—*E.D.*
LONG ISLAND, NEW YORK
5Y

• • • • • • • • •

A VERY NICE THING WE DID A FEW TIMES on our honeymoon was splurge . . . whether it was skipping the el cheapo tapas bar and opting for a fancy dinner, or renting a car instead of taking five trains and a small ferry to get to our destination. On our honeymoon, we tried hard to remember that this was our time to be decadent and that we deserved to pamper ourselves a little (not an easy task for two generally level-headed, frugal people).

—*DANA HAGENBUCH*
SAN FRANCISCO, CALIFORNIA
2M

Have your hair done the way it usually looks. I hate it when the bride is unrecognizable because their hair is so over-done.

—*DEB*
ORONO, MAINE
32Y

THE BEST PART OF OUR WEDDING was the second "dance" at the reception. My family is white, Mormon and very conservative. His is black, Jamaican and also conservative. We played the song "We Are Family," and the DJ told everyone at the reception who was in any way related to the two of us to come and dance. It was so amazing— with so many different colors, shapes, clothing styles and ages, we were all boogying down to the music and laughing and having a blast. There was no alcohol at all, so it was truly just us being silly and completely opening up as a new family.

—K.R.
NEW YORK, NEW YORK
7M

● ● ● ● ● ● ● ●

““An older guest at our wedding gave us this advice: 'Through it all, be kind to each other.' So far, this advice has worked well!””

—BONNIE
NORWALK, CONNECTICUT
12Y

● ● ● ● ● ● ● ●

NEVER GO CAMPING FOR YOUR HONEYMOON. You don't want to have to shuffle off to the woods to take care of business. Even if you are the outdoorsy type, your honeymoon should offer the option to have breakfast delivered to you in bed. Go on that Alaskan camping trip some other time.

—DAVID COHEN
SAN CARLOS, CALIFORNIA
7Y

BRING CLOTHES THAT COVER UP your entire body, even if you're going to a tropical location. On our honeymoon, we went snorkeling in Maui. A jellyfish stung my arm, leg and stomach, which hurt like crazy. Even worse, because I'd only packed tank tops and sundresses, I had to walk around all week with this huge scar on my arm. It looked like I'd been whipped, and believe me, my husband and I heard all sorts of jokes about that.

—*S.A.*
LAKE FOREST, CALIFORNIA
6Y

IF YOU GO TO A SUN-DRENCHED, Caribbean island, bring sun block! Slap it on as soon as you walk outside. They are not joking when they say you will burn in an hour or less. I didn't heed that advice and paid a great price. It undermines the purpose of your honeymoon when your spouse's slightest touch leaves white marks on your reddened skin.

—*JANICE*
CINCINNATI, OHIO
35Y

BOOK YOUR HONEYMOON WAY IN ADVANCE. My husband and I arranged everything for our honeymoon to Hawaii at least six months ahead of time. Not only did this give us time to shop around for better deals, but it cut way down on stress. Whenever the wedding work would start piling up, we could look at pictures of the beaches and talk about our upcoming vacation. This was the fun part.

—*CANDICE PORTER*
OVERLAND PARK, KANSAS
1Y

WHERE TO GO ON THE HONEYMOON

I THINK THE HONEYMOON SETS THE MOOD for the marriage to come so you have to pick the right place to go. It should be somewhere new to both of you, just like your new marriage. We went to Hawaii. We had a blast, and I really think that it built up momentum for the rest of our marriage.

—KEVIN L. MCCARTHY
PITTSBURGH, PENNSYLVANIA
30Y

• • • • • • • • •

MY HUSBAND AND I CHOSE BERMUDA because of the beautiful weather, flowers, water, beach, calm, quiet. We felt happy and proud to be there after pulling off a 200-person wedding! And we had more than one cook in the kitchen at our wedding—and I don't mean the caterer—so we really appreciated being away from people.

—JULIA RONTHAL
BERKELEY, CALIFORNIA
11Y

• • • • • • • • •

EVERY COUPLE HAS TO DECIDE FOR THEMSELVES what they are interested in doing on their honeymoon. Many people encouraged us to plan a romantic honeymoon in which we would spend two weeks basically "gazing into each other's eyes." We would have been bored after the first day! Instead, we traveled around Spain and Portugal learning about history, architecture, the people, and the languages. We were pretty busy, but we learned a lot about each other and the countries we visited.

—MEREDITH E.
FAIRFIELD, CONNECTICUT
5Y

• • • • • • • • •

ON OUR HONEYMOON, WE SPENT MORE TIME in planes than exotic islands. They should make exotic planes and boring islands for people like me.

—B.P.
ORLANDO, FLORIDA
3Y

YOU ONLY HONEYMOON ONCE. Go all out. We lived like total rock stars for a week in Baja at Las Ventanas al Paraiso in Los Cabos, Mexico. We stayed in a rooftop luxury suite that was $4,000/night. We used a bit of money that we received as wedding presents, but primarily had set aside a special honeymoon fund after our engagement. It was worth every one of those 900 million dimes. We went horseback riding and picnicked on the beach, drove around in a jeep, had breakfast served to us, had a limo at our disposal. I married the greatest woman in the world. I'm grateful to have those memories with her.
—M.K.
SAN FRANCISCO, CALIFORNIA
5Y

. . . .

WE WENT TO COSTA RICA ON OUR HONEYMOON. We wanted an eco-adventure. We saw lots of monkeys. One even grabbed a lizard and ate it like a candy bar.
—AMANDA
ATLANTA, GEORGIA
2Y

. . . .

MOUNTAIN BIKE RIDING IS AN ACTIVITY that my husband and I enjoy together, so we incorporated that into our honeymoon. But for the two months leading up to the wedding I hadn't touched a bike—too many details and distractions—so when we started riding in New Zealand, I was really feeling it in my rear-end! My husband and I joked about it all week, because walking like you've been in the saddle translates well to other seemingly appropriate honeymoon activities.
—ANONYMOUS
MONTEREY, CALIFORNIA
5Y

MARRIAGE HAS MEANT MORE TO ME than I had ever expected—something changed the day we made this lifelong commitment of love and friendship to each other. I used to agree when people said it was only a piece of paper and how could it make a defining difference? But I have experienced so much more than that. We both felt a spiritual presence on our wedding night, as if we were being wrapped together with some invisible thread. It's hard to explain—let's just say it was the best sex ever!

—ANONYMOUS
 PALO ALTO, CALIFORNIA
 2Y

The First Year: Settling Down With Your New Spouse

J ust look at you: Still sunburned and sighing every three minutes, thinking of your new spouse. Welcome to marriage. It's just the beginning of a great ride. And it starts with the first year of conjugal bliss. Some couples will tell you it was the most challenging time in their union; others will get starry-eyed just thinking about it. Regardless of how you experience it, we've got the advice to get you through.

PEOPLE TREAT YOU DIFFERENTLY WHEN you're married, like you've just joined this elite club or something. First off, you don't have to answer the "So when are you getting married?" question anymore. Thank heavens!

—BARBRA ANNINO
    MCHENRY, ILLINOIS
    4Y

BELIEVE EVERY-ONE WHEN THEY SAY THE FIRST YEAR IS THE HARDEST. IT'S TRUE!

—TASHA
    LOUISVILLE,
    KENTUCKY
    1Y

THE HONEYMOON WAS OVER very quickly, probably about a month after we got married. I don't know how it is for other people, but we fought over EVERYTHING— from finances to how to fold the towels. Our first year was definitely a learning curve. There were a lot of moments when I asked myself if I had made a mistake, but we've both learned a lot and I love him.

—*NIQUIE RAGLAND*
NASHVILLE, TENNESSEE
3Y

· · · · · · · · ·

AT SOME POINT EARLY ON IN A MARRIAGE I think it's a good idea for the two of you to sit down and write down some long-term goals. Focus on when you'd like to start having children and how many to have. Look at where you want your careers to go. Discuss home-buying plans and how it will be paid for. Take into account all the major events you expect to encounter. You can always change plans later, but it's good to have a starting point.

—*WALTER HUGHES*
CLEVELAND, OHIO
45Y

· · · · · · · · ·

What's mine is mine and what's his is mine. Just kidding. We share every-thing—except bed space.

—*JESSICA*
SARASOTA, FLORIDA
3Y

THE FIRST YEAR OR SO IS WHEN couples set the stage for their entire marriage and the norms and habits they establish now may last a lifetime, such as who does what around the house, etc. When I first married 22 years ago, I wanted to be a perfect bride and did all the cooking and clean-ing. To this day, my husband has never cleaned a toilet or run a load of wash. Changing him at this point is too difficult. Changing myself is hard, too, because I'm used to doing these tasks and don't want to go to the trouble of "training" him.

—*ANONYMOUS*
DENVER, COLORADO
22Y

WE DIDN'T REALLY STRUGGLE OR FIGHT, and I feel like our honeymoon period lasted for several years. Because we were honest with each other and we knew how to have fun outside of the bedroom as well as in it, we have had a very easy time of it compared to most couples we know.

—*JENNIFER G.*
ROCK HILL, SOUTH CAROLINA
4Y

. . . .

"You're no longer an individual. You're no longer two individuals. The two become one. We operate and think together as a team. Her desires are my desires. My desires are her desires."

—*CHRIS GRAHAM*
SYRACUSE, NEW YORK
9Y

. . . .

PART OF THE FUN OF BEING MARRIED is that you know that you have someone to share all your good news with and someone who will call you first with their good news. When my husband got his first promotion at work six months after we were married he called me first—not his mother. That was something I made sure she was aware of later.

—*BRITTANY TALIAFERRO*
MEYERSDALE, PENNSYLVANIA
2Y

INTRODUCING PETS . . .

INTRODUCING OUR PETS AS HOUSEMATES was fun. My husband had a dog named Chloe, who is half Doberman, half German Shepherd, and was a rescue dog. I've got a little male Dachshund who is very Type A and used to being the King of the house. We hoped they'd get along, but had no idea what to expect. Soon enough we realized that when they were left in the house alone while we went to work, Chloe acted as though my dog was her puppy, and they adore each other. They are friends for life—they have as much of a relationship as Wayne and I.

—*MARSHA H. DONAHUE*
CAPE ELIZABETH, MAINE
1Y

• • • • • • • • •

THE BEST THING WE DID IN OUR FIRST YEAR was getting our puppy (a pug), because it showed us that we could successfully take care of something together. We'd sit in bed at night with the dog and just talk for hours while playing with it — it was so special to do something like that together.

—*NATALIE*
EVANSTON, ILLINOIS
8Y

MAYBE IT SOUNDS HOKEY, but I think it's important to tell yourself that you have, and will continue to have, the marriage you've always dreamed of. The chances are, if you bring a loving attitude to your marriage and don't sweat the small stuff, your marriage will be fantastic.

—*DARCY*
RIVERSIDE, ILLINOIS
14Y

• • • • • • • •

AFTER THE WEDDING AND HONEYMOON are over, many couples feel let down, even depressed. When a couple returns home, I recommend taking two weeks of "bliss time." Share your wedding photos with your friends, have romantic dinners, and sprinkle flower petals on the bed. Don't sweat things too much for those two weeks.

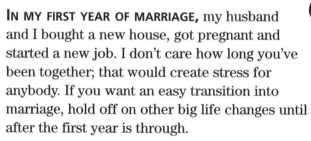

—*SHARON NAYLOR*
MADISON, NEW JERSEY
6Y

• • • • • • • •

IN MY FIRST YEAR OF MARRIAGE, my husband and I bought a new house, got pregnant and started a new job. I don't care how long you've been together; that would create stress for anybody. If you want an easy transition into marriage, hold off on other big life changes until after the first year is through.

—*DEBBIE REDDEN-BRUNELLO*
TEMECULA, CALIFORNIA
15Y

BLACKOUTS AND SNOW DAYS take on a whole new meaning when you're a newlywed. We were snowed home from work without electricity, so we just made our own sparks. It was one of the best days of our first winter together, and we didn't go anywhere or do anything (at least not anything that we can talk about in public!).

—CARL M.
MINNEAPOLIS, MINNESOTA
1Y

. . . .

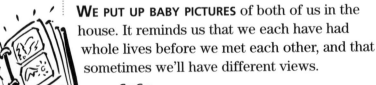
Commit random acts of kindness. Also, the occasional compliment or soft kiss on the forehead goes far.

—CHRIS POMEROY
ATHENS, GEORGIA
1Y

. . . .

I TRY TO THANK HIM FOR taking on responsibilities, especially ones that I might have done, but that he did to help me out.

—ANONYMOUS
LOS ANGELES, CALIFORNIA
11Y

. . . .

WE PUT UP BABY PICTURES of both of us in the house. It reminds us that we each have had whole lives before we met each other, and that sometimes we'll have different views.

—CEECEE
RENO, NEVADA
7Y

WHEN WE CELEBRATED THE FIRST YEAR of marriage it was so exciting. My husband was the type who everyone thought would never settle down, but seeing us make it through a whole year was the best thing ever—we took a trip to Vegas and had a carefree weekend without worrying about anything going on at home.

—JEAN ROBERTSON
GLENVIEW, ILLINOIS
4Y

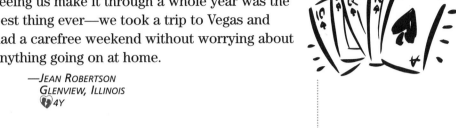

MY HUSBAND AND I LIVED SEPARATELY for the first 5 months of our marriage, and then we finally moved together into a cozy 2-bedroom apartment. Shortly after we moved in, we got a call from one of his old fraternity brothers, who said he needed a place to stay for a week or so. Of course, my husband said yes, and we rearranged our spare bedroom to accommodate our new arrival.

Unfortunately, the week lasted three months! He was a really nice guy and had been in our wedding party, so we had a hard time turning him away, but after a while, we realized he really had to go. It was the first real "situation" that my husband and I had to deal with as a married couple, and looking back, we both agree that it was the right thing to do and we are glad that we dealt with it the way we did.

—M.
BIRMINGHAM, ALABAMA
12Y

TALK. WE LOVE TO TALK. I swear that's why we got married. We can talk about anything. And we'll talk about it for hours.

—COURTNEY ALFORD-POMEROY
ATHENS, GEORGIA
1Y

Be realistic! Newlywed couples are less likely to experience deep declines in marital satisfaction if they have a realistic picture of their relationship—even if that picture is not completely rosy.

—HEALTH DAY NEWS

MOVING IN: BEFORE OR AFTER IT'S OFFICIAL?

I REMEMBER WHEN WE MOVED INTO the same house. It was my husband's place, and we were renting. I've always been very independent. He picked out a room and said, "I know that you need your own space, so this is your room to do whatever you'd like—office, retreat, whatever." I appreciated that so much. It's important to realize what the other person needs when you're combining two households. It helps to have your own space.

—*LINDA BOWER*
LOVELAND, COLORADO
14Y

. . . .

TWO MONTHS AFTER I WAS ENGAGED, my fiancé and I bought a house. We fought daily about paint colors for the walls, what couches to buy, who was doing more work than the other person and who was paying for what. It was terrible, but I knew that if we could make it through that, we'd be fine in the long-run. It's good practice for marriage.

—*KELLY VENERE*
SPRING GROVE, ILLINOIS
5M

. . . .

WE LIVED TOGETHER FOR 8 MONTHS before we were married, and I thought that would prepare us, but it didn't. We fought a lot that first year. It was very hard. I think we realized that it was for real—that we couldn't walk away. We fought about money, where we were going to live, careers. We had to learn to fight and stay together.

—*ALISON WEISS*
HALF MOON BAY, CALIFORNIA
17Y

MY HUSBAND AND I DIDN'T LIVE TOGETHER before we were married. I think this made our first year of marriage more difficult—we were learning to be married and learning to live together at the same time. He had moved into my apartment, though we bought a house fairly soon afterwards. That was mainly because my husband got tired of hearing me say, "This is *my* apartment." Once we argued about him getting his own dresser drawer! Looking back on it, I still wouldn't have lived with him prior to getting married—but I *should* have given him the drawer.

—K.K.
LONG BRANCH, NEW JERSEY
4Y

. . . .

WITHIN ONE WEEK OF HIM MOVING IN, almost every room had a TV in it, except the living room, where I said "hands off." It's my sanctuary, where I read.

—MARSHA H. DONAHUE
CAPE ELIZABETH, MAINE
1Y

. . . .

WHEN MY HUSBAND AND I GOT MARRIED, we immediately moved into a brand-new place together—rather than me moving into his apartment or him moving into mine. This helped us see things as "ours" rather than "mine" or "yours" right away. Everything was new—our house, our friends, our jobs—so it felt natural to start our new identity as a couple.

—WENDI K.
PARKER, COLORADO
15Y

1) Laugh a lot, love uncondi-tionally and don't keep score.
2) Always make him think it was his idea.

—*Rachel Ruvo*
Chapel Hill,
North Carolina

It **doesn't matter how long** you've been dating. Once you get married and move in together, you'll learn new things about your spouse. Be prepared: you won't like all of these new things. It turns out my husband has an annoying habit of getting up in the middle of meals to answer phone calls, though he never did this while we were dating. Years later, we're still working on the compromise solution.

> —*Dani*
> *San Francisco, California*
> 7Y

• • • • • • • • •

Say **"thank you" a lot.** Tell your spouse he did a great job fixing the lock, painting the door, cutting the lawn—whatever. Bake his favorite cake. Make sure there's always ice cream and milk in the refrigerator. Never make a "couple" commitment without first checking with your spouse.

> —*Jan Alder*
> *Atlanta, Georgia*
> 7Y

• • • • • • • • •

Take **the longest trips you can** after you first get married—the rougher, the better. My husband and I took several months to backpack and camp around the West during our first year together, and we got to a whole new level of understanding each other. At first, we fought a fair amount, especially because we were with each other 24/7. But then we just really got it—how to deal with each other, compromise, sense the other's unspoken needs. We've been married many years, but we still think that those first few months did more to solidify our relationship than the several years of dating we'd done before that.

> —*J.D.*
> *Baltimore, Maryland*
> 6Y

I **STILL REMEMBER OUR FIRST FIGHT** as a married couple. My husband and I had just moved into a new house, and he hired a contractor to do some outside work. I remember walking into the front yard and giving my opinion about how something should look. I was basically told that the inside of the house was mine to decorate, and the outside was his. I walked away in a huff; I will never forget that fight. We typically lump the genders into roles: He mows the lawn, she does laundry. But these stereotypes aren't always accurate. Sit down with your mate and have a discussion about what parts of the house are most important to you before moving in.

—*DEBBIE REDDEN-BRUNELLO*
TEMECULA, CALIFORNIA
💗*15Y*

HONEY, REMEMBER OUR PET SCORPION?

When my wife and I were first married, we lived in a trailer in a bad part of Northern Texas, and I had a huge phobia of bugs. One morning, I woke up at 4:30 and saw a 4" scorpion on my left shoulder, waiting to strike. I started freaking out and trying to kill it with my combat boot. The entire time, my wife was laughing. As an apology for making light of the situation, she agreed to wake up at 4:30 the next morning and cook me breakfast. When she opened the refrigerator, however, there was another 4" scorpion staring back at her. Terrified, she grabbed a can of Raid and a steak knife and proceeded to kill it. We moved out of that dump soon afterward, but we also learned something valuable: The importance of laughter.

—*MARK SCOTT*
SAFFORD, ARIZONA
💗*17Y*

DURING OUR FIRST YEAR OF MARRIAGE, we moved from Maryland to Michigan, bought our first house, adopted two puppies and started new jobs. Somehow, though, none of these new things and life struggles have changed our marriage. If anything, we feel stronger and closer knowing that we're going through life together.

—*AMANDA*
GRAND RAPIDS, MICHIGAN
💔*1Y*

. . . .

WE HAVE THIS COLLECTION OF little crystal things on a shelf over the toilet. Right after we got married and moved in together, I was in the living room and suddenly heard this jingle of the bell. Even though we'd never talked about it, I just knew she was giving me a signal, so I got a roll of toilet paper and brought it to her. She did, in fact, want paper, and when she saw that I had it in my hand, she just cracked up. The two of us were laughing so hard. We suddenly felt like we were really on the same wavelength and that we were really and truly married, like one of those old couples who practically read each other's minds.

—*JOHN KIM*
LOS ANGELES, CALIFORNIA
💔*6Y*

. . . .

NO MATTER HOW BADLY THINGS in a marriage may go later on, the first year or so is usually pure magic. Ask anyone. You're still riding that dating high and then you add in the opportunity to play house with someone you love. It's so new, exciting and different than living with your parents. I think even if you were married to a serial killer you'd be in 7th heaven for that first year.

—*SANDRA FENKOWA*
SILVER SPRING, MARYLAND
💔*3Y*

OUR FAVORITE THING TO DO TOGETHER is be silly. We make inanimate objects talk. Our most recent "character" is a small salt-and-pepper shaker that we got on the plane on the way back from our honeymoon. For some reason, it's adorable and hysterical to us. We have a laundry list of private jokes—that are probably not even remotely funny to anyone else—but can crack us up for hours.

> —DANA HAGENBUCH
> SAN FRANCISCO, CALIFORNIA
> 2M

• • • • • • • •

WE TRY TO MAKE SURE WE HAVE MOMENTS of connection every day, where we acknowledge each other. We send romantic e-mails to each other at work. My husband will send text messages to me from the airport when he's traveling. Or when he set up my new cell phone, he programmed it to say "Hi Lover" when the screen comes on. We constantly remind each other how much we love each other.

> —KRISTIN SWEETSER
> REDMOND, WASHINGTON
> 13Y

• • • • • • • •

START FRESH . . . WITH EVERYTHING. Consider marriage like moving to a foreign country, because it is. Find a new place together. Do not move into one of your already existing homes. Sort through your things and choose the ones that work best. You don't need three microwaves. Give the extras away. Start your new life with as little clutter as possible.

> —J.M.D.
> NEW YORK, NEW YORK
> 5Y

Most newlyweds experience a brief emotional bounce after their wedding, but they eventually return to the same outlook they had on life before they tied the knot.

—CNN

FIRST YEAR ON THE ROAD

When we were a young married couple, camping fit our budget and our time schedules. I was teaching first grade and my husband was going to college. During the first 7 years of our marriage, we spent many happy hours setting up the pup tent, blowing up air mattresses, zipping our Coleman sleeping bags together, and developing outdoor cooking skills. We drove a Chevrolet Corvair in many directions over the course of 7 summers.

My favorite trip was a 10-week road trip from Joliet, Illinois to California, where we camped the entire time. It was the summer before we moved into our first home. We budgeted $100 a week (this was in 1973) and the only credit card we had was Standard Oil.

We headed out Route 66 in the middle of June and stayed at many state parks and recreation areas along the way. We had the luxury of time on this trip. If we liked a camping area, we stayed a few days. I remember waking up everyday with anticipation of the adventure and wondering what new places and things we would discover.

We always found some little ice cream place along the way, so we adopted our own special rule on this trip: ice cream for lunch. We met and talked to people from all over the country during night-time campfires and we both got to see so much of this beautiful country—the Grand Canyon, Sequoia, Yosemite, Kings Canyon, Sante Fe, Taos and Salt Lake City were just some of the highlights. Ultimately, though, the best part of the trip was being together for every moment of those 10 weeks, sharing, discovering and having the time of our young married lives.

I think it was that trip that solidified our marriage. We are going to celebrate our 37th anniversary this December and we still love to see new places together. Our motto has become "always keep a bag packed."

—DEE
OAK LAWN, ILLINOIS
36Y

OUR FIRST YEAR OF MARRIAGE was a real challenge. The day after we got married, we moved into a co-op living situation in Washington, DC with 5 other people. In other words, we had zero privacy. We did it primarily for financial reasons, and privacy became all about timing. We didn't find private places, but private times. There were occasions when we knew everyone was out, and we would lock all the doors, set the alarm, and pretend it was our own huge house. Living with the group forced us to bond in a way that has served us well over the years. The following year, we finally moved out and into our home, which made for a glorious time, and even more reason to celebrate. Once we settled in, we spent a lot of time around the house naked, simply because we could.

> —*SCOTT A. MOORE*
> *EISLEBEN, GERMANY*
> 🖤*17Y*

• • • • • • • •

THE FIRST YEAR WAS HARD. There were definitely not candles and roses all the time, though we continued making efforts to be romantic regularly. I think it would have been better if we'd started out thinking, "How do we have to arrange our lives so that we're meeting each other's needs?" instead of "How can we be just like other successful couples we know?" It's all about fine-tuning and balancing what is necessary for each spouse to be ultimately happy. I tried to convince myself that there was a perfect mold for marriage but really, I had to create my own.

> —*WHITNEY JASINSKI*
> *RENTON, WASHINGTON*
> 🖤*3Y*

Some varieties of marriage: polygamy, polygyny, endogamy, exogamy, common law marriage, monogamy.
—*ABOUT.COM*

GET AT LEAST *SOME* NEW FURNITURE together as you decorate your house. Even if you have what you need by combining stuff, buy something small. We threw out both of our coffee tables, got a new one, and added some throw pillows to the couch. It was just nice to have something that had no memories for either one of us except for the memories we were making together.

—*LUZ*
SAN DIEGO, CALIFORNIA
15Y

If you ever get married and you decide to live at your parents' house, don't! It doesn't work.

—*W.D.O.*
ATHENS, GEORGIA
4Y

• • • • • • • •

GIVE, GIVE, AND GIVE. Avoid criticism at all costs. Show appreciation all the time. Remember a primary goal of marriage is to heal the wounds of childhood and each person needs to be understood from that perspective. Only by having compassion and providing a safe environment with open communication can love grow.

—*A.N.P.*
PITTSBURGH, PENNSYLVANIA

• • • • • • • •

TO ALL WOMEN: Men will forever be interested in sports. Just because they want to watch sports on TV doesn't mean they don't love you or care about your day. If you learn this right away it will save a lot of fighting.

—*GERRY*
CHICAGO, ILLINOIS
3Y

• • • • • • • •

LEARN TO SPEAK HIS LANGUAGE! I'm American. My husband is Belgian. I learned French so that I could understand him better. It really impressed his parents, too!

—*WENDY*
MIAMI, FLORIDA
8M

DON'T LEAVE YOUR SINGLE FRIENDS OUT of your new married life. You'll be the one who loses out in the end. After the rush of being a newlywed wears off, you won't always want to be around your husband, and you'll want to go do fun things with just your girlfriends. Other married friends might be hard to drag out, especially once they've got kids. And your single friends are the ones you'll want to turn to!

> —C.H.
> LOS ANGELES, CALIFORNIA
> 💔 10Y

• • • • • • • •

DON'T FORCE YOUR HUSBAND to live in a flowery, girly house. My poor husband suffered in silence for years till he finally admitted he hated the bedroom, and that it totally turned him off. He joked that that was why we always had sex with the lights off. We went out and bought a more neutral set that we both liked, and we started keeping the lights on!

> —JILL H.
> NEW YORK, NEW YORK
> 💔 15Y

• • • • • • • •

UNTIL YOU GET MARRIED, you may not have seen this person at their absolute worst, like when they just got home from work after a rough day and an even rougher commute. It's when you try to see where the other person is coming from and learn to accommodate each other's moods that you accept your spouse's flaws and realize that you have some of your own that he's dealing with as well.

> —LINDSEY GAWRON CALDWELL
> ARLINGTON, VIRGINIA
> 💔 1Y

MY HUSBAND ALWAYS TOLD ME that it is better in marriage for two people to be focused on a common aim rather than on each other. If the focus is just on each other, you will always find imperfections, but if it's a common aim, you can focus on perfection.

—*S.B.*
KERALA, INDIA
14Y

• • • • • • • •

THE NUMBER 1 QUALITY TO HAVE in the first year is patience. Things aren't going to go well all the time. People get too impatient with one another. Both of you eventually are going to mature and grow up, and you'll know how to avoid arguments over tiny, menial, stupid little things.

—*GENE GREEN*
COLUMBIA, SOUTH CAROLINA
34Y

• • • • • • • •

IT IS CRITICAL TO MAKE TIME to be together no matter what. We had so many commitments and were pulled in so many directions the first year between our jobs, our families and our other responsibilities that we actually had to *schedule* time to be together.

—*A.M.*
PASSAIC, NEW JERSEY
14Y

• • • • • • • •

I THINK IT'S IMPORTANT TO MAKE FRIENDS as a couple, and make sure you all like each other. I have had some friends that my husband didn't particularly care for and he had some that I felt the same way about, but you have to work it out. It's good to have other couples to hang out with.

—*ANONYMOUS*
PACE, FLORIDA
42Y

MAKE TIME FOR EACH OTHER. Make sure your wife knows you take the marriage seriously and are commited to sharing more of yourself, your own life, your interests, your friends. Get involved, together, in a community. Support networks are essential to long-term family and marital success. And don't be afraid to argue—it's not the end of the world, it doesn't mean your marriage was a mistake. It just means you need to air some concerns and, ideally, come to a common understanding.

—*DAN DUPONT*
ARLINGTON, VIRGINIA
7Y

Marriages are most fragile in the early years, with 20% of divorces occurring in the first 5 years of marriage.

—*NEWLYWED DEBT*

• • • • • • • •

TEACH YOUR HUSBAND HOW TO COOK. It's a fun thing to do together—kind of sensual, actually. I taught my husband how to make several things and every once in a while he decides to make us a fantastic meal. Or sometimes we cook together. Either way, it makes him proud. It gives me a break. And it's romantic for both of us.

—*S. COLEMAN*
NEW YORK, NEW YORK
4Y

• • • • • • • •

IF YOU THINK, "MARRIAGE SHOULD BE like this," you're doomed to failure. It's like taking a boat out to sea and making up your mind that you will have great weather. Then a storm comes along and you refuse to acknowledge that it's raining. You have to roll with the changes and surrender your preconceived notions of what marriage could be and should be, and you have to work as a team.

—*MIKE G.*
ATLANTA, GEORGIA
3Y

KEEPING OLD FRIENDS

IF YOUR SPOUSE DOESN'T LIKE SOME of your old friends, then go see them without your spouse! You don't all have to get along. It's good to get out separately.

—*R.A.*
AUSTIN, TEXAS
♥*3Y*

• • • • • • • •

THE WEIRDEST PART IS HOW YOU SUDDENLY STARTED hanging out with other couples. And when friends tell you they're getting married, you get all excited, because you start to think about hanging out with them long term. It's a whole new friendship ballgame.

—*COURTNEY ALFORD-POMEROY*
ATHENS, GEORGIA
♥*1Y*

• • • • • • • •

KEEPING OLD FRIENDS GETS HARDER AND HARDER as time goes by. Don't be afraid to make new friends, but be best friends with your spouse. We like to think we don't necessarily need anybody else. It gets harder and harder to have "friends" with everything else going on in our lives. We have work acquaintances and people to barbecue with and whatnot, but not a whole lot of true friends beyond each other.

—*JAMES*
FRANKFURT, GERMANY
♥*5Y*

• • • • • • • •

WE BOTH CURRENTLY HAVE ONE GOOD FRIEND of the opposite sex. It can add to the relationship. I feel a little competition on some level. But it's good to have opposite-sex friends. I find men more interesting. Women can be too emotional and boring.

—*SALLIE*
JOHNSON CITY, TENNESSEE
♥*10Y*

IT IS NICE TO HAVE FRIENDS WHO YOU'VE KNOWN for a long time. In a way, they become your extended family. Plus, it's wonderful to know someone who remembers you young, fit and beautiful. They still see you that way.

—JANICE
CINCINNATI, OHIO
35Y

• • • • • • • •

ACCEPT THE OTHER PERSON'S FRIENDS AND PREVIOUS LIFE. I didn't realize how important my husband's friends were to him until after we got married. He still travels with them on a "guy weekend" once a year. And he talks to them on the phone regularly. I didn't know that I would have to share my husband with them, but they're a "package deal." Luckily, I like them, too!

—MEREDITH E.
FAIRFIELD, CONNECTICUT
5Y

• • • • • • • •

ONE OF OUR BEST FRIENDS IS one of my husband's old girlfriends. Years ago, I might have felt a little threatened by it, but that's long since faded.

—ANONYMOUS
LOS ANGELES, CALIFORNIA
11Y

DURING THE FIRST YEAR OF MARRIAGE, it would drive my husband crazy when he came home from work and there would be one little thing out of place. But I went out of town a few times and when I came back the house was a total disaster. It made me realize that I did not have a major "messy" flaw, and that when left to his own devices, my husband was worse than me. I called him on it, and he has since learned that life is better when you don't take every little thing so seriously—and that he is not perfect either.

—*L.*
WEST NEW YORK, NEW JERSEY
4Y

* * * * * * * * *

EACH PERSON SHOULD KEEP THEIR OWN interests. I'm really into yoga, and that's something I do without him. It's wonderful to have a place to go where I am not half of a couple; I'm just my own whole person.

—*E.*
SAN FRANCISCO, CALIFORNIA
6Y

* * * * * * * * *

"A man in love is incomplete until he has married. Then he's finished."

—*ZSA ZSA GABOR*

WHEN WE STARTED DATING, my wife still was friends with an ex-boyfriend. But I didn't like it and she gave it up. Women have this idea that they can be friends with guys they've slept with. But men just don't think and feel the way women think and feel. A man stays in touch with a woman but it's with the idea that there's a chance of sex. And women think they've got a friend. I've seen it happen many times.

—*ED GILMORE*
CARLTON, GEORGIA
4Y

TRAIN YOUR HUSBAND RIGHT AWAY to keep the house the way you want it. For example, if you don't like something (say, dirty dishes in the sink), make a big deal of it right away and don't let him get away with it. If you start the marriage out by letting him know how you want things to go, it will be easier to train him.

—*ALLISON ENGLANDER*
NORTH BRUNSWICK, NEW JERSEY
3Y

. . . .

ESTABLISHING A WEEKLY ROUTINE is definitely a good thing. If you're both working 9-5 jobs, then it allows you time to eat dinner together and talk about the day, which is definitely important in your first year of marriage when you're establishing yourself as a couple.

—*JAYME*
O'FALLON, MISSOURI
4M

. . . .

THE MOST IMPORTANT THING a married couple needs are relationships with other married couples. When you have open relationships with other marrieds, you'll realize that a lot of the troubles you're going through are common. Early in our marriage, my husband and I didn't have close relationships with other married couples. We fought a lot, and we used to feel very alone in our problems. We didn't know what to do. We didn't have anyone to talk to. Now, when I see young married couples, the ones who seem the happiest are the ones with close relationships with other married couples. They realize that their problems aren't unique, that people can work through their problems.

—*GRACE*
LIVERPOOL, NEW YORK
21Y

OUR FIRST YEAR OF MARRIAGE REVOLVED around a lot of disappointments, a thin paycheck and a baby with colic. It was not the sweet refuge either of us had imagined and I know I cried more than laughed during that time. But what kept us going was dreaming, always looking "outside the box" for a better way, making tiny little moments seem rich with romance or sentiment. Our first Christmas, we only had enough money for a Christmas tree. We decorated it and sat in the dark in the evenings, thinking of future holidays when the tree would be accompanied by gorgeously wrapped gifts and memories. Ever since, we keep the spirit of Christmas alive as a reminder of where we came from and how abundant our life is, regardless of money.

—A.H.
HIGHLAND, NEW YORK
24Y

• • • • • • • •

WHEN MY WIFE AND I FIRST GOT MARRIED I remember thinking all day at work that I couldn't wait to get home to see her. It was like that was the only thing I thought about. I felt so lucky to know that no matter how bad my day was she'd be there when I got home. That's an incredibly wonderful feeling.

—STEVEN A. PARSONS, JR.
FT. ASHBY, WEST VIRGINIA
1Y

• • • • • • • •

DURING THE FIRST YEARS OF OUR MARRIAGE, I had a really tough time sharing my personal living space. It was a period of adjustment for both of us in many ways.

—JEANNIE SPONHEIM
LOVELAND, COLORADO
10Y

TIME WAS THE MOST DIFFICULT THING to learn to share. We had both been single for a while and didn't really have to consult with anyone else before making plans. It didn't take long, but there is a definite adjustment period when you learn to check with your better half before inviting people over for dinner or accepting an invitation.

—JAN ALDER
ATLANTA, GEORGIA
7Y

* * * * * * * *

YOU NEVER FIND OUT ABOUT SOMEONE UNTIL you live with them on a day-to-day basis.

—BONNIE LAMB
CHICAGO, ILLINOIS
14Y

* * * * * * * *

WE'RE TAUGHT THAT WE'LL FIND OUR SOUL MATE and it will last forever and we'll go crazy every time they walk in the room. But that's not true. You find a totally different level of love in marriage, even in the first year. Wanting to feel that first love forever is like wanting to be 16 again. You can remember what it was like and enjoy it when it's happening, but you have to let it go. You can't be 16 again. It's the same with love. And it doesn't mean the relationship is over if the love changes.

—DEB S.
SAN DIEGO, CALIFORNIA
27Y

Don't Forget To:
1. Honor your vows.
2. Show love through action every day.
3. Affection, admiration, appreciation and fondness— express them.
4. Share your lives with each other.
5. Enjoy companionship.
6. Keep romance alive.
7. Remember, you are a team.
8. Manage your personal stress.
9. Apologize quickly, and forgive.
10. Learn how to resolve conflict.

—GIRLS & BOYS
TOWN

DURING THE MAGICAL "HONEYMOON PHASE," when you see the world through rose-colored glasses, your perfect sweetheart can do no wrong! But when that phase ends, don't despair. That's when the real relationship begins. When you discover that your once-perfect mate has glaring, nagging faults, you have a choice to make: Do you end the relationship—either emotionally or by leaving —or do you keep loving this person anyway? If you choose to hang in there and love your spouse, faults and all, you take the marriage adventure to an exciting, grown-up level. Working through challenges and joys together can bond the two of you to the point where nothing—and nobody—can come between you! That kind of togetherness is definitely worth the effort.

—*GRACIELA SHOLANDER*
FORT COLLINS, COLORADO
15Y

Can You Hear Me Now? Communication and Other Challenges

Sure, you love your spouse. But sometimes he or she can make you so mad! We know. We've heard hundreds of stories about arguments—what causes them, what ends them, and tips on getting through them. Ultimately, it comes down to communication. You can speak loudly, or you can speak softly. Regardless, you have some things to resolve. We're here to help. Read on.

I THINK FRIENDSHIP IS MOST IMPORTANT in marriage, because if you have a strong friendship with your spouse then you will treat them with respect, truly love them and take care of them. Everything else follows.

> —ANONYMOUS
> NEW YORK, NEW YORK
> 💘 1Y

HAVE AN EXCELLENT SENSE OF HUMOR.

> —ANNE KUBAS
> DANVILLE, CALIFORNIA
> 💘 29Y

WHEN YOU ARE FIGHTING, don't ever get up and leave the house, or the room, for that matter. There is nothing more disrespectful than someone getting up and leaving. Marriage is about communication, and if you leave the room, you are saying to the other person, "You aren't worth communicating with." That defeats the whole purpose of marriage.

—DAVID KARL
NEW YORK, NEW YORK
4Y

• • • • • • • •

FIND YOUR CONVERSATION PLACE: I've discovered that the best place for my husband and I to talk is while we're lying in bed hugging. Sure, we talk at other times and in other places, but our very best talks are usually there. I recommend that couples find where they have their best heart-to-heart talks. It's helpful to know this because when there's a time that you need to talk things over, it may be a good idea to save the talk until you're at your special conversation place.

—ANONYMOUS
READING, PENNSYLVANIA
4Y

• • • • • • • •

WE'VE BEEN TO A COUPLE OF DIFFERENT conferences about communication. When we're really pissed off at each other, we use this "Speaker-Listener" magnet. When one person has the magnet, the other person has to listen to what they have to say, and then repeat back what they heard to make sure they understand properly. Then you pass the magnet. That actually works pretty well.

—JAMES
FRANKFURT, GERMANY
5Y

YOU KNOW WHEN THERE IS SILENCE and lack of eye contact, it's time to talk, to look each other in the eye and get to the bottom of something. You can't let it fester. It's important to be sensitive and not stuck in a routine so much you don't notice subtleties.

—*MEL MOLINO*
MILL VALLEY, CALIFORNIA
20Y

MOST IMPORTANT QUALITY IN A MARRIAGE? Communication! My husband is a journalist so he does his best communicating in writing, which I've learned to accept. It works very well now since he travels so much. E-mail really helps. Sometimes, writing one's feelings is much easier and more effective than speaking them.

—*NANCY*
BRUSSELS, BELGIUM
40Y

" I suggest you close the windows and communicate openly. Keep your fights between you. "

—*ANONYMOUS*
BROCKTON, MASSACHUSETTS
4Y

BEST QUALITY IN A HUSBAND? Good listener. I never realized how important it was to be with someone who really listens. My husband always makes me feel like there is nothing more important than what I have to say.

—*NAN B.*
WILLIAMSBURG, VIRGINIA
34Y

COOPERATION AND RESPECT ARE THE KEYS. If there is a disagreement, it's settled out of mutual concern for resolving the issue. It's cooperation, not compromise. Compromise sounds like you're accepting something less than what you want.

—*HUGH FOLEY*
STILLWATER, OKLAHOMA
10Y

• • • • • • • •

GET AN OLD COIN TO KEEP AROUND the house. Someone gave us an antique silver one when we got married. If you ever have an argument, and you can't come to a solution, flip the coin. Whoever wins wins the argument.

—*LEE MONTOPOLI*
RIVER DALE, NEW JERSEY
6Y

• • • • • • • •

WE BOTH HAVE A FIRM BELIEF THAT we should always exhibit the utmost respect for each other. That is huge with us. Even in our everyday, mundane interactions, we try to act as though we are "company." There will be times then when it's hard to say, "Would you please . . . ?" but I've found that it helps to let go of the little, petty tensions and angers of our daily lives.

—*DEB S.*
SAN DIEGO, CALIFORNIA
27Y

• • • • • • • •

I THINK OUR MARRIAGE IS SUCCESSFUL because we get each other's humor. I'm not sure we even have the ability to be serious when we need to be. We can, in a humorous way, talk to each other when we're really not pleased with each other and still get the message across.

—*J.C.*
ALEXANDRIA, VIRGINIA
3Y

Pointer: Argue naked.

—*RICHARD HALL*
KENNESAW,
GEORGIA
10Y

THOSE THREE LITTLE WORDS

WE SAY "I LOVE YOU" ALL THE TIME and probably I say it too much. But I say it honestly because that thought pops into my mind when I get close to him. If you don't say it to your spouse at least once a day, it's a mistake.

> —*J.H.*
> *ATHENS, GEORGIA*
> 5Y

YOU SHOULDN'T SAY "I LOVE YOU" TOO OFTEN because it almost certainly means you are insecure.

> —*PATTY LAMBROPOULOS*
> *LAKE FOREST, ILLINOIS*
> 25Y

DON'T FORGET TO SAY "I LOVE YOU" EACH TIME you leave each other and every night when you lay down to sleep. It's important to keep saying it and hearing it. I don't think hearing my wife say those three little words will ever get old.

> —*RON COLAGUORI*
> *CLEVELAND, OHIO*
> 10Y

FOR ME, I CANNOT HEAR "I LOVE YOU" ENOUGH, and it's because I know my husband means it. Do I count the times we say it in a day or week? No. But we say it as often as we can. Those three words can lift a person in an instant.

> —*KRISTEN MILLER*
> *WINTERVILLE, GEORGIA*
> 1Y

THE MAIN QUESTION IS, how do you *not* take personally something that the person who means more to you than anyone else in the world says to you? I'm afraid I don't handle it too well.

—*JERRY*
EAST NORTHPORT, NEW YORK
❤20Y

• • • • • • • •

BE THICK-SKINNED WITH YOUR SPOUSE. He or she is going to say or do something to hurt your feelings or upset you. On the flip side, be aware that what YOU do has the ability to hurt your spouse, and no one wants to do that.

—*M.J. TWETTEN*
CHICAGO, ILLINOIS
❤2Y

• • • • • • • •

BE AWARE THAT SOME OF THE MOST divisive and bitter arguments occur in the car. Take a page out of Peter Pan and think happy thoughts when you're driving somewhere with your spouse. Resist the urge to comment on driving ability, sense of direction, whether you're late or early, etc. Something about that close proximity, closed space and

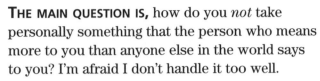

lack of witnesses brings out the worst in people and married couples are especially susceptible.

—*ALLISON BURKE*
ARLINGTON, VIRGINIA
❤15Y

The other 69?
69% of disagreements that arise in a marriage are never resolved.

—*THE WALL STREET JOURNAL*

UNDERSTAND YOUR SPOUSE'S NEEDS: One night when my wife was sick, resting on the couch, she asked me to get her some cantaloupe. I just didn't feel like cutting it up, so I got her something else. She didn't like it and we got into an argument that seemed never-ending. Since that day, quite a few discussions and much soul-searching later, "Hey, I need some cantaloupe" has become our catchphrase for "You're not giving me what I need." It's an inside joke that my wife and I share, and it's helped to diffuse many an argument since then.

> —CRAIG
> BETHLEHEM, PENNSYLVANIA
> 9Y

• • • • • • • •

CHOOSE YOUR BATTLES. Every time my wife and I start to argue, I think to myself, "Is it really worth it? Or should I back down now and fight for something I really believe in." Usually, it's not worth it.

> —LEO
> ATLANTA, GEORGIA
> 21Y

• • • • • • • •

WE LIVE BY POST-IT NOTES. He doesn't remember half of what I tell him. And he doesn't hear the other half! If you want the message received, write it down.

> —SUETTA GRIFFITH
> FISHERSVILLE, VIRGINIA
> 39Y

• • • • • • • •

IF THINGS GET REALLY HARD, take some time off. Meaning, go out with friends and take a little break. You want to get out of the situation before you say something mean or overreact.

> —SUE
> WESCHESTER, NEW YORK
> 14Y

Respect and patience are the keys to making a marriage work.

> —P.W.
> CHICAGO, ILLINOIS
> 10Y

WHEN YOU FIGHT, DON'T HIT BELOW THE BELT. Try to remain calm and respectful. Also, don't start off your side of the story with "you"—"You do this, you don't do that." Instead, start it off with "I feel . . . " "I feel like I'm not being heard" works a lot better than, "I feel like you don't listen.'"

—*JOANNE*
CHICAGO, ILLINOIS
♥ *22Y*

❝Friendship, respect and passion—it's like a three-legged stool. Without any one of them, you'll fall.❞

—*DAVID WIENER*
NEW JERSEY

SHOW RESPECT FOR YOUR SPOUSE when you go out with other couples. It's embarrassing to see married people snipping at each other publicly. I know my husband's not perfect, but I always try to make him seem that way in front of other people. Whatever problems we have, we deal with in private.

—*BARB ZAHN*
FRANKTOWN, COLORADO
♥ *48Y*

YOU MUST LEARN HOW TO RESOLVE CONFLICTS well. You must learn to disagree in a fair and healthy way. We had to learn this the hard way.

—*JENNIFER B.*
YARDLEY, PENNSYLVANIA
♥ *5Y*

TOLERANCE AND THE ABILITY TO GET past arguments, no matter how trivial and ridiculous they may seem, is a golden key to surviving your marriage. My wife and I have been together for more than 40 years because we've simply refused to let hurdles and problems hurt our marriage. During one argument, my wife grabbed me by the arm, threw me into the bathroom and locked the door from the outside. I had nothing else to do, so I decided to take a nice hot bath. I was in the tub for nearly an hour before she unlocked the door and asked what the hell I was doing. I'll never forget the look on her face when she saw me relaxing in the bath. She had spent the last hour on her hands and knees scrubbing the kitchen floor, and here I was soaking in nice warm and soapy water.

— *ANONYMOUS*
LONDON, ENGLAND
44Y

• • • • • • • •

NEVER BERATE YOUR SPOUSE, even in jest. It is difficult in the heat of anger, but saying something negative to your partner because it makes YOU feel better will come back to bite you later on, either in the guilt you feel or that slightest bit of trust your partner lost for you.

— *SHEENA KROCK*
KUNKLETOWN, PENNSYLVANIA
3Y

• • • • • • • •

WHAT DO WE ARGUE ABOUT? Baby duty and baby doodie. How do we resolve it? I do a half-ass job, but with a lot of feeling, and repeat until she feels sorry for me.

— *B.P.*
ORLANDO, FLORIDA
3Y

"To keep your marriage brimming, with love in the loving cup, whenever you're wrong admit it; whenever you're right shut up."

—*OGDEN NASH*

DON'T EVEN *THINK* IT: THINGS TO AVOID

NEVER LEAVE A SITUATION MAD. Never storm out of a house. Never leave unfinished business, even if you've got to be late for something, because you've got to come back home at some point. Some things take three minutes to settle. But if you leave before you settle, you're going to argue for three days.

> —*TIM MURPHINE*
> *VALDOSTA, GEORGIA*
> 4Y

• • • • • • • •

NO NAME CALLING, EVER. No leaving the house. You can walk outside, go into another room, but don't "leave." It causes too much insecurity in the other person and will build resentment. No bringing up past transgressions, unless this is the exact same issue.

> —*STACI PRIEST*
> *PFLUGERVILLE, TEXAS*
> 6Y

• • • • • • • •

DON'T GO TO BED MAD. My husband and I have stayed up until 3 a.m. some nights over the years, talking things out. But I believe to this day that it's important to resolve things before solidifying them in sleep.

> —*W.F.*
> *MERTZTOWN, PENNSYLVANIA*
> 22Y

• • • • • • • •

DON'T EVEN ALLOW YOURSELF TO THROW the word "divorce" around. You have to work through your differences. You made the commitment and you have to honor it. Learn not to stay mad at each other. All the problems ultimately make for a stronger marriage.

> —*TERRI MASTELL*
> *PETERSBURG, OHIO*
> 24Y

DON'T HOLD A GRUDGE WHEN FIGHTING. We let it all out, find out where the difference of opinion is and then respect the difference and that's it. No one agrees on everything—face it.

> —JOHN
> MORTON GROVE, ILLINOIS
> 40Y

. . . .

MY HUSBAND MADE A RULE EARLY ON in our marriage: No fighting in the bedroom. The bedroom is a place for love and romance, not fighting.

> —ANONYMOUS
> LIVERPOOL, NEW YORK
> 13Y

. . . .

MAKE SURE TO RECOGNIZE AND ACKNOWLEDGE that you are different people and you don't have to agree on everything. I used to think my wife didn't like me when she'd disagree and worried about her leaving me for someone who believed exactly the same as she did. It took a while for me to learn that we didn't have to see eye to eye to still love one another.

> —DAVID LELAND
> SAN DIEGO, CALIFORNIA
> 1Y

. . . .

LEARN WHEN TO FIGHT, AND WHEN NOT TO. Time of day and circumstance dictate this. My wife tends to wake up mad at me, so I've learned not to argue with her at night. Instead, I try to get my point across early and let her ruminate on it for the rest of the day. By dinnertime, hopefully she'll realize I'm right.

> —DOUG BRIMMER
> COLORADO SPRINGS, COLORADO
> 13Y

ALWAYS BE WILLING TO LISTEN TO YOUR SPOUSE.
Take a deep breath and say, "OK, you have
something to say, I want to hear it."

—*K.E.*
LOVELAND, COLORADO
💔*18Y*

● ● ● ● ● ● ● ●

MY HUSBAND IS A TERRIBLE LISTENER! I used to
find myself talking to him, but realizing that I was
actually talking to myself because he wasn't listening. That made me furious! Then I decided on
a plan of action. If there is something that I really
want my husband to hear, I tell it to my children.
And they tell him. He always listens to them.

—*N.*
HOUSTON, TEXAS
💔*19Y*

● ● ● ● ● ● ● ●

A GUY GETS OUT OF THE DOGHOUSE BY waiting
until she tells him that he's out of it. Just go
through your day and wait until you're notified
that your punishment is over. You're not the one
who decides how long you are punished. So take
your damn spanking.

—*MIKE G.*
ATLANTA, GEORGIA
💔*3Y*

● ● ● ● ● ● ● ●

NO LEAVING THE PREMISES, though breaks from
the conversation are allowed. My husband used
to drive off when he was pissed at me. That is
not acceptable.

—*ALYSSA AGEE*
SNOQUALMIE, WASHINGTON
💔*7Y*

**If your wife
isn't speaking
to you, don't
interrupt.**

—*H.L.*
NEW YORK,
NEW YORK
💔*17Y*

YOU'VE GOT TO LEARN TO PUT YOUR WIFE in the doghouse. I've seen too many couples where it's "the woman's always right, the man's always wrong" stereotype. I put my wife in the doghouse early on, when appropriate. One person shouldn't always be wrong or be subservient.

—*TONY T.*
SAN FRANCISCO, CALIFORNIA
4Y

• • • • • • • •

COMMUNICATION, I HAVE FOUND, is by far the most important skill in marriage. All of our disagreements involve misunderstandings that could be resolved with better communication. This is something worth working on. I repeat what he is saying, to be sure I understand. Often I think I know, but I find I did not.

—*ROSEMARY C.*
MONTVILLE, NEW JERSEY

• • • • • • • •

MY HUSBAND HATES IT WHEN I CRITICIZE his driving. He gets upset. He's just really bad in traffic; he beeps his horn and calls the other drivers names. They can't hear him, but I have to listen. So when we're in a car, on a long trip, I do crossword puzzles and make sure not to look at the road.

—*M.L.R.*
AVERILL PARK, NEW YORK
44Y

Take a little time to cool down after a heated argument. But within an hour, have a "reconciliatory conversation."

—*THE WALL STREET JOURNAL*

A PROFESSIONAL OPINION: COUNSELING

DON'T BE TOO PROUD TO GET HELP: This may seem like such obvious advice, but if you come upon hard times, go see a counselor. My husband and I went through a really dark time in our marriage a few years ago. Our counselor taught us how to communicate effectively, and our marriage is so much stronger because of it.

> —*KRISTEN*
> *BETHLEHEM, PENNSYLVANIA*
> 9Y

DON'T GIVE IN TO COUNSELING; I think it's the easy way out. If we're having a problem, my wife always suggests counseling because "all her friends are doing it." I think it's pointless to pay someone to solve your problems when you can just sit down and talk them out ourselves, which usually works anyway.

> —*S.*
> *BUFFALO GROVE, ILLINOIS*
> 14Y

COUNSELING, COUNSELING, COUNSELING. Counseling! Even if you think it's stupid, it's important to talk out your thoughts. You may be thinking 3 kids. He might be thinking 10. You may be thinking 2 careers, and he's thinking stay-at-home-mom. We've done counseling a couple of times. It's good to have someone to mediate.

> —*CHERYL NORTON*
> *WASHOUGAL, WASHINGTON*
> 16Y

IT'S CRUCIAL THAT YOU COMMUNICATE. Don't clam up. If you can't talk about it, then get help and go to a couples' counselor. Don't be afraid of the stigma. It works.

> —*R.A.*
> *AUSTIN, TEXAS*
> 3Y

IF YOU AND YOUR SPOUSE CAN'T REACH RESOLUTION on an important issue, get a third party to arbitrate. We were so stuck on a decision we had to make with our child that we called our school's psychologist, explained the dilemma, and she suggested a new solution that made us both happy.

—*M.C.*
DENVER, COLORADO
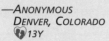*25Y*

· · · · · · · · ·

IF THE SINK GETS CLOGGED, you call a plumber. If you break your leg you call a doctor. With emotional things, you think you know how to fix it and you don't. We went to a wonderful counselor, and I think she saved our marriage.

—*J.E.*
PORTLAND, MAINE
20Y

· · · · · · · · ·

THE SECRET TO A GOOD MARRIAGE IS THERAPY. I'm not kidding. Most couples don't have the skills to identify their issues or know how to begin to work through them. I think a couple of sessions of marriage counseling every year should be mandatory for couples who want to stay together, like an annual check up. A good therapist will help you sharpen your communication abilities and problem-solving tools. Make your marriage healthier.

—*ANONYMOUS*
DENVER, COLORADO
13Y

The truth
hurts: Most
arguments
experienced
by married
couples cannot
be resolved.

—JOHN M.
GOTTMAN, PH.D.

THE HARDEST PART OF COUNSELING IS that you
really can't avoid conflict and arguing during the
process. That can be very difficult if one of the
reasons you're there in the first place is because
you don't open up and communicate in order to
not have a fight. Heated discussions will ensue.
And that's OK and, sadly, necessary. You just have
to talk through things in a grown-up fashion.

—DAVID HUBBELL
KIRKLAND, WASHINGTON
8Y

MY HUSBAND IS NOT INTO COMMUNICATION. A lot
of times he is very defensive. We do best when I
bring an issue up by e-mail. Meanwhile, doing
Pilates keeps me from going to bed angry.

—ISABELLA
SANTA CRUZ, CALIFORNIA
3Y

KEEP IN MIND THAT USUALLY WHEN communication
goes wrong we make this strange assumption
that there is malice. But remember, there is no
malice. You married this person. You just have to
find a way to understand each other. There are a
lot of ways to make that happen.

—DEB
ALPHARETTA, GEORGIA

IF I'M PARTICULARLY HURT OR ANGRY about
something, I write a letter to him so I won't go
on and on about the same thing but I'll be to the
point. Those letters, like in person, end with my
positive feelings about him and our relationship.

—MONICA Y. DENNIS
BRIDGEPORT, CONNECTICUT
3Y

JUST BECAUSE YOU HAVE A HUGE FIGHT doesn't mean you're going to break up.

> —*D.S.*
> *BOSTON, MASSACHUSETTS*
> 6Y

. . . .

" After 16 years of marriage, the greatest thing we have ever done is to have family meetings every week. We plan everything together—the grocery list and menu for the week, the recipes, and the schedules for each person. Then, the kids know what to expect, and everyone works together. "

> —*ANONYMOUS*
> *DENVER, COLORADO*
> 16Y

. . . .

"YOU'RE THE ONE WHO . . . " is the key phrase that lets you know when things are not going well in a conversation with your spouse. That phrase is always used when you have started to cast blame. When my husband and I hear it, it usually makes us laugh. We don't say it very often anymore.

> —*CHRISTINE C. GODIN*
> *SAN ANTONIO, TEXAS*
> 20Y

I WAS RAISED IN A FAMILY WHERE I never heard my parents argue and was not used to confrontation. One day, I was so upset with my husband that after he left for work I spent all day crying. By the time he got home, I blurted out how mad I was. He had no idea anything was wrong, because I hadn't told him what was bothering me. His response was that I needed to learn to speak up for myself if I wanted things to improve. Let's just say I took his words to heart so much that today my husband jokes that he wishes he'd never taught me to speak up, because now I'm so vocal!

—JOAN K. HITCHENS
CENTENNIAL, COLORADO
40Y

•　•　•　•　•　•　•　•

HAVE A FRIENDSHIP WITH YOUR SPOUSE. A lot of couples don't communicate and don't have anything to talk about. My husband and I had a special daily ritual. Every day at 5:00 we had a cocktail, and we'd talk, and then we'd have a second drink at 5:45. That time was our time. It was fun and relaxed. We started with bourbon and water and then graduated to vodka and grapefruit juice in our later years. The alcohol probably loosened our tongues.

—ANONYMOUS
PARIS, MISSOURI
53Y

•　•　•　•　•　•　•　•

NEVER FIGHT TO WIN, FIGHT TO RESOLVE. All couples have disagreements. If people fight to one-up the other it is very unhealthy, but if you fight to resolve on equal terms, it will be all right.

—J.P.
HOBOKEN, NEW JERSEY
9Y

AS YOUR MARRIAGE MATURES, you'll be surprised how your attitudes about doing things for your spouse changes, too. My husband is involved in a men's group, and over the last two years, there were several deaths. The group decided they wanted to have a seminar with experts on preparing for death and end-of-life issues. My husband really wanted me to do this with him. It was an all-day affair, there was homework we were supposed to do before the event, and it was being held far from our home. The timing couldn't have been worse for me and I did everything I could to avoid it. Usually, he's very easygoing, but this time he didn't back down. After all this time together, I trust and respect that there is stuff he knows about me, and that sometimes he sees things in situations that I don't. In the end, it was this phenomenal experience.

—*JILL ZIMMERMAN*
ISSAQUAH, WASHINGTON
24Y

• • • • • • • •

WHEN THE FIGHT ISN'T IMPORTANT, it helps sometimes just to let the other person be right even if you don't believe it.

—*LANAN SHELTON*
AUSTIN, TEXAS
37Y

• • • • • • • •

NOT EVERYBODY IS GOING TO COMMUNICATE the same way or at the same time. In our marriage, I'm the morning person. She isn't. And you have to understand that. I sort of wake up jabbering, ready to go—but with my wife you have to let her get her feet under her first.

—*HERB GRIFFITH*
FISHERSVILLE, VIRGINIA
39Y

People ask us, "Who wears the pants in the family?" My answer is, "We both wear shorts."

—*BRIAN L. COY*
EL CAJON,
CALIFORNIA
25Y

Phrases that
let your
partner know
you're listen-
ing and want
to hear more:
• "Go on."
• "Please
continue."
• "Keep it
rolling."
• "Let me hear
all of it."
• "Keep
talking."
• "It's still your
turn."
—FROM "COUPLE
TALK"

REAL LOVE IS REAL WORK. Sometimes it's easy and it's romantic, and sometimes you wonder why you married them and then you have to push through those feelings and do what's best for that person anyway.

—MONICA Y. DENNIS
BRIDGEPORT, CONNECTICUT
3Y

FOR YEARS, MY WIFE WAS substantially overweight. After 8 years of marriage, I finally let her know how I felt—that I was worried about her health, that it seemed to me that she didn't care about her appearance or about the way I thought she looked. This was not a Hallmark moment. Anger, tears, the works. But in time we realized that a confrontation had been necessary to deal with a very real problem, and we learned how important it is that we both feel comfortable expressing our feelings, no matter what.

—ANONYMOUS
MADISON, WISCONSIN
12Y

FORGIVENESS IS A HUGE PIECE OF MARRIAGE. It's about being selfless. It sounds really good and it looks good on paper. But living it, oh. That's much different.

—MARY JACKSON
STILLWATER, MINNESOTA
37Y

 ARGUING IS NOT WHAT BREAKS UP a marriage—not making up will. Do not let pride get in the way of saying, "I'm sorry."

—DION LOERTCHER
SALT LAKE CITY, UTAH
7Y

CODE WORD: LAUGHTER

MY HUSBAND AND I DO WHAT WE CALL "the right dance" when either of us is right and the other is wrong. This tends to break the tension!

> —*LISA NASEEF*
> *PORTLAND, MAINE*
> 14Y

ONE LITTLE TIP FOR YOUNG MARRIED COUPLES is to find a sentence or a detail or a word that can act as a code for ending a quarrel. Early on in our 33-year marriage, Brooks and I were ranting at one another about some truly insignificant issue, and I blurted in frustration, "I just do not understand you!" Brooks looked off in the distance, and said after considerable delibera-tion, "I am an enigma." Well, we both just began laughing uncontrollably at the pomposity of his statement. Now, when we are wrangling and one of us has had enough, we pull out the old line and laugh as always. When you laugh together, arguing ceases to become possible.

> —*JEANIE GODDARD*

HOW TO DEFUSE AN ARGUMENT: One time my husband and I were having an argument. For some reason, maybe out of frustration, my husband suddenly made this really strange sound: "Meep!" What made it even funnier was that he said it in this really high-pitched voice. He sounded so silly, I started to laugh, and the argument quickly defused. From then on "Meep!" has been our code word for, "OK, I surrender. This argument has gone on long enough. Let's stop it already!"

> —*A.K.*
> *ALBERTIS, PENNSYLVANIA*
> 7Y

THE ONLY WAY MY HUSBAND AND I have survived these past 9 years is through prayer, commitment and endurance, in that order. Marriage is not just a trial session of which you can say, "I love you" one day while warm tingling feelings invade you, or daydreams distract you, and then when trouble arises you give up. It's a commitment and hard work.

—*B.L.S.*
CHEYENNE, WYOMING
❤ *9Y*

. . . .

❝If we have an argument and it's going south, we stick our tongues out at each other. We make a face. I mean, there are issues that you have to deal with. But that helps keep it from getting out of hand.❞

—*BOB G.*
VIRGINIA BEACH, VIRGINIA
❤ *25Y*

. . . .

ALWAYS KISS BEFORE GOING TO SLEEP at night, even if you have quarreled. Someone has to make the first move so don't let pride get in your way.

—*ISABEL*
BERKELEY HEIGHTS, NEW JERSEY
❤ *MORE THAN 50Y*

REMEMBER THAT EVERYONE NEEDS TIME for themselves even when they're married. Perhaps especially when they're married! My husband works long hours every day and has a long commute by car to and from work. So, when he gets home, he goes straight up to his favorite room and listens to his stereo. It helps him to unwind and relax. He only needs thirty minutes. Then he helps the kids with their homework and we have some time together.

—*SUE*
DESTIN, FLORIDA
27Y

• • • • • • • •

SPACE IS A GOOD THING. You have to have alone time to spend by yourself or with friends.

—*J.D.*
ATLANTA, GEORGIA
5Y

• • • • • • • •

I UNDERSTAND THAT IN EVERY ARGUMENT my wife and I have had in our more than 40 years of marriage, I was right and she was wrong. Still, being perfect in an imperfect world, I know I need to adjust to my wife's far-less-than-perfect behavior. After one bruising battle dealing with a potential world-altering decision, which was over the purchase of a small table, we were furious with each other. Being perfect, I did the perfect thing. I went to the florist, bought her a cactus plant, and wrote on the card: "Because you're so prickly." She dissolved in laughter.

—*DOUGLAS S. LOONEY*
BOULDER, COLORADO
41Y

Duck! Forty percent of women say they have hurled footwear at a man.

—*WWW.EXPAGE.COM*

I READ SOMEWHERE THAT YOU'LL BE in more trouble if you're right and your wife is wrong than if you're wrong and your wife is right. Because of this, I almost always let my wife be right.

—*EMMILLIO E.*
VANCOUVER, CANADA
33Y

My husband says if you have to work hard on your relationship, you don't have a good marriage.

—*BATIA ELKAYAM*
LOS ANGELES,
CALIFORNIA
29Y

LISTEN, THEN LISTEN SOME MORE. You can never, never listen to your spouse enough. Think carefully before you utter a single word. At the same time that you're thinking, keep listening.

—*ROBERTA BEACH JACOBSON*
KARPATHOS ISLAND, GREECE
14Y

I LOVE WHAT ERMA BOMBECK SAYS to the husbands: "Do you have the patience with her that you have with your biggest client who puts you on hold?" And to the wives: "Do you have the same pride in his achievements that you felt when you got the mold off the grouting in the shower?" The longer we are married, the more in danger we are of taking each other for granted and we should make sure that never happens.

—*PATSY CRUSE*
HOUSTON, TEXAS
35Y

DON'T LOSE YOUR SENSE OF HUMOR. When you're angry with your spouse, remember how you felt about him/her when you first fell in love. The pleasant memory will temper your (temporary) anger.

—*K.K.*
FALMOUTH, MAINE
35Y

MY WIFE AND I ARE CELEBRATING 35 years of
marital bliss this year. But in our early years, we
had to work out some listening/communications
issues. My wife would come in from work every
day, complaining about this or that in the
workplace. Inevitably, she would end her session
of venting with "What do you think about that?"
I would then offer my opinions. One day, she
finally said to me, "You always end up giving me
advice. I just want you to listen." Now I listen—
and although she still may ask me, rhetorically,
what I might think, I nod and sometimes mirror
what she says. The routine works great.

> —*ARMANDO DIAZ*
> *BURLINGAME, CALIFORNIA*
> 35Y

. . . .

I JUST REPEAT TO MYSELF, "SHE'S RIGHT, she's right,
she's right."

> —*ANONYMOUS*
> *LONG VALLEY, NEW JERSEY*
> 35Y

. . . .

I HAVE LEARNED THAT IF THE GRASS IS GREENER on
the other side, that couple probably has a higher
water bill. No marriage is easy. I always wanted
my marriage to be exactly like the fairy tale
marriage I thought my parents had. What I didn't
know was that my parents had their ups and
downs, too. My parents hid a lot from their
children in order to create an ideal childhood for
their children. In turn, I felt inclined to copy their
idyllic relationship. I am truly grateful to them for
my upbringing, but I also had a lot to learn about
the reality of marriage.

> —*ASHLEY ADAMS*
> *MANHEIM, PENNSYLVANIA*
> 3Y

NEVER HAVE AN IMPORTANT DISCUSSION when
you're both hungry.

—*MARIANA*
SAN FRANCISCO, CALIFORNIA
13M

• • • • • • • • •

FIND TIME FOR YOURSELF. Since I got married later
in life, I was quite independent and comfortable
being alone. I do enjoy spending time with my
husband, but I also need to have time to myself,
and taking that time regularly is important to
maintain marital bliss and my sanity!

—*JAYNE J.*
TULSA, OKLAHOMA
13Y

The Money Pit: Figuring Out Your Finances

Money might make the world go 'round, but it stops some marriages cold. If you get a handle on how to deal with it, your marriage will be that much happier. And someday, you and your spouse might finally have that house you always dreamed about. Some couples believe in putting everything together; others prefer to keep some money separate. Either way, here are some tips on how to balance your checkbook—and your marriage.

IN 38 YEARS OF MARRIAGE, my husband and I have never once fought about money. How is this possible? We simply haven't made getting ahead financially our top priority.

—*JANIS HACKETT*
CENTENNIAL, COLORADO
38Y

CAN'T WE JUST WIN THE LOTTERY ALREADY?

—*EMBER NEVILL*
FT. WORTH, TEXAS
2Y

AH, MONEY. HAVING IT IS ALWAYS BETTER than not having it, but your life shouldn't be all about making more of it. When we were first married, we had two careers, two incomes, and made a decision to save one income and live on only one. Four years after we were married, we were able to put a down payment on our first house, and ultimately I was able to choose to stay home when we had children, since we had already learned to live on one salary. That is not always possible in today's economic times, but it's really important to decide together how you want to live your life. Clarify what your priorities are going to be, whether it's a trip every year, or saving for your children's education, or buying a bigger house. Whatever your goals are, you need to discuss them and make sure you agree on how to achieve them.

—*JANICE*
CINCINNATI, OHIO
35Y

. . . .

NOTHING CAN RUIN A MARRIAGE FASTER than a mortgage, and money matters on the mind can mess up the marriage bed. Don't mortgage your marriage; live within your means.

—*E.N.*
NEW YORK, NEW YORK
48Y

. . . .

DO THE BILLS TOGETHER. Work on the budget together and make decisions about money together. Figure out how each of you is programmed to spend money and then find a middle ground. Find a money management tool that works for you.

—*JAMES*
FRANKFURT, GERMANY
5Y

YOU WILL CELEBRATE THE DAY that the mortgage is paid like you will celebrate no other day in your married life. Live it up on that day. You've earned it.

—*MEGAN TANNER*
WHEELING, WEST VIRGINIA
💔 19Y

• • • • • • • •

SHARE EVERYTHING, NO MATTER WHO makes more money. This is a partnership and you both contribute value, whether financial or not. Make sure you each have spending money. Be clear about debt and what's okay and what's not. Be upfront about debt you bring to the marriage and about your credit—this is VERY important to your future together. Agree on your short term and long term financial goals. Don't agree to anything you really don't want to do financially.

—*R.A.*
AUSTIN, TEXAS
💔 3Y

• • • • • • • •

THE MOST DIFFICULT THING WE'VE FACED in our marriage was combining our finances. Money was pretty tight when we first married. We didn't balance the checkbook the same way and we didn't agree on what to pay first or who should get more money. It was a big lesson in how to compromise, share control, and most importantly, how to give and take.

—*ED GILMORE*
CARLTON, GEORGIA
💔 4Y

• • • • • • • •

WE GOT ON THE SAME CELL PHONE PLAN. In fact, we don't even have a land line now.

—*LISA HABIB*
ATLANTA, GEORGIA
💔 1Y

Come to daddy when you need some coin!

—*B.P.*
ORLANDO, FLORIDA
💔 3Y

HAVE A SMALL AMOUNT OF MONEY that can be used by either of you for anything—buying a sweater, going to a ball game, paying to see a show with friends, whatever.

—*SUSAN M.*
CHICAGO, ILLINOIS
8Y

• • • • • • • •

" If you have more going out than coming in, this causes a lot of stress on a relationship. We have tried to keep these words of wisdom in mind during our 41 years of marriage. We have never been rich in material belongings but have remained rich in love. "

—*VELDA AND KENNETH BODKIN*
LOVELAND, COLORADO
41Y

• • • • • • • •

SET ASIDE SOME MONEY FOR EACH of you to donate to causes you find worthwhile. We discuss most of our donations, especially big ones, but we have a small amount of discretionary money for our own personal causes.

—*ELLIS*
SEATTLE, WASHINGTON
4Y

WHEN YOU ARE FIRST MARRIED and times are financially tight, look at it like this: there is no reason to fight about something that you don't have. If you want to fight, fight about your ugly couch or your unsightly wallpaper. At least those things exist. Fighting about a lack of money is like picking on your husband for not being taller. Fighting isn't going to change either one of those things.

—*MITZIE HAGEN*
WHEELING, WEST VIRGINIA
💔*16Y*

• • • • • • • •

DON'T GET CAUGHT UP IN NEEDING new things. Defer your gratification a little bit. It's hard to do in our culture. You don't have to ask me if you can go buy a CD, but if you're going to buy a refrigerator, we need to consult with each other.

—*DEB S.*
SAN DIEGO, CALIFORNIA
💔*27Y*

• • • • • • • •

USE PAYROLL DEDUCTION FOR SAVINGS. Force yourself to do it. It becomes painless and you get used to not having it. You don't miss the money, and you're building up a nest egg or an emergency fund. And if you get a raise, increase your savings deduction.

—*J.V.*
RANDOLPH, VERMONT
💔*14Y*

There is evidence that couples' financial problems (including debt) are linked to increased levels of stress, conflict, and marital duress as well as decreased levels of marital satisfaction.

—*JOURNAL OF MARRIAGE AND FAMILY*

WILL THAT BE ONE CHECKBOOK OR TWO?

EVERY MARRIED WOMAN SHOULD HAVE her own savings account that her husband doesn't know about. My ex-husband would not have been able to pull the things he did if I'd had access to a little cash.

> —*M.P.*
> *SARATOGA SPRINGS, NEW YORK*
> 12Y, 5Y

* * * * * * * *

IF ONE PERSON IN A MARRIAGE IS A LITTLE EDGY about spending, is a saver, maybe you should have separate bank accounts. Otherwise, you just have to be patient when they start acting like you only have a quarter left in your checking account.

> —*K.J.*
> *WICHITA, KANSAS*
> 7Y

* * * * * * * *

I AM A BIG PROPONENT OF USING ONLY ONE CHECKING ACCOUNT. It's supposed to be one for all and all for one, right? You are both in the marriage together and you should share everything—especially the money. Having separate accounts can only lead to squabbles and mistrust. Don't do it.

> —*MARY WEBB*
> *WHEELING, WEST VIRGINIA*
> 21Y

* * * * * * * *

JOINT BANK ACCOUNTS ARE EXTREMELY IMPORTANT. In our case, money goes into a "pool" that we use to pay off everything. It also establishes the thought that we are working as a team in the house to pay off bills and purchase new things. This way, I can never look at my wife and say "that's mine" or "this is yours"—everything we own is ours.

> —*LEE*
> *LAKE VILLA, ILLINOIS*
> 1Y

DON'T HAVE SEPARATE BANK ACCOUNTS; it is just one more thing that can separate a married couple.

—*ANONYMOUS*
ANN ARBOR, MICHIGAN
10Y

• • • • • • • •

IT CAN BE TOUGH TO DEAL WITH BUDGETING if one spouse stays home to take care of the kids and doesn't earn money—especially if they're a real shopper like my wife is. She'd always worked and was used to being able to spend freely, but we had to be much more careful with only one salary and extra mouths to feed. I recommend setting up a separate account that is the stay-at-home spouse's to use as she pleases. In our case, it reduced my stress a lot because I knew there was a limit to her spending ability, and it also reduced her stress because she could buy things without asking my permission.

—*S.M.P.*
PORTLAND, MAINE
14Y

• • • • • • • •

WE HAVE JOINT BANK ACCOUNTS, but separate checking accounts and that has always worked for us. Some couples I know have "his" and "hers" money and it just complicates things. If I want to go shopping or get my hair done, the money will come from my checking account.

—*HELEN*
MORTON GROVE, ILLINOIS
40Y

• • • • • • • •

HAVE ONE JOINT ACCOUNT AND TWO SEPARATE. That way you don't have to explain what you bought. I am a saver and my wife's a spender. This arrangement saves us a lot of arguments and fighting.

—*DAVID*
HASLET, TEXAS
7Y

BUY A HOUSE AS SOON AS YOU CAN stretch yourself to do it financially. It will be a bit difficult to afford in the beginning, but what will happen is that your finances will grow and in a few years it will be comfortable. A few years after that, you'll probably want to move into a bigger place anyway because of kids. In the meantime, you'll have built up equity in the house. It forces you to save money.

> —FRANK
> RENO, NEVADA
> 7Y

. . . .

No matter how much you have, it won't be enough.

—D.W.
ATLANTA, GEORGIA
8Y

JOINT CREDIT CARDS ARE NOT FOR EVERYONE. Even though I trust my husband very much, I don't need to see how much he spends on a suit or on a night out with his friends. We ran into trouble with this and I blew up when I saw that he spent over $1,000 on a suit for work when I cringe to spend $100 on a pair of jeans. Some things just don't need to be out in the open because it causes more problems.

> —NATALIE
> EVANSTON, ILLINOIS
> 8Y

. . . .

BUYING GOOD QUALITY THINGS—furniture, appliances, etc.—will cost more in the short term, but you have to remember that you are in this marriage and life together for the long term. We shelled out more money for really nice furniture and energy-efficient, quality appliances, and it has meant fewer repairs and replacements over the years. We're convinced we've saved money in the long run.

> —DEKE
> SAN DIEGO, CALIFORNIA
> 15Y

AS MUCH AS YOU PLAN, you never really know when that first baby is going to come along. It's a good idea to be as prepared as you can so that you could get pregnant at any time. Think about how having a child will affect your career and your household finances. It's better to be prepared and have a good idea of how you'll be able to deal with it when it does happen.

> —*HELEN HUGHES*
> *CLEVELAND, OHIO*
> 💔 *40Y*

• • • • • • • •

WE LOST A TON IN THE DOT.COM CRASH. We've had to cut back, do with less. Now we save for the future; you can't assume there will be somebody to take care of you down the line.

> —*MEL MOLINO*
> *MILL VALLEY, CALIFORNIA*
> 💔 *20Y*

• • • • • • • •

ELOPE! With the money we saved from not having a formal wedding, we were able to put a sizable down payment on our first apartment. Our parents also gave us nice cash presents, since they saved on not having to pay any wedding expenses. Three years later, we sold the apartment for 4 times the amount we bought it for! And because of the big initial down payment, we were able to save with our smaller monthly mortgage payments. We just celebrated our 6th anniversary and now live in a fabulous house on a lake, which we were able to afford because of the profits on the sale of the apartment and our 3 years of savings. We strongly recommend eloping!

> —*SHAZ G.T.*
> *PACKANACK LAKE, NEW JERSEY*
> 💔 *6Y*

I SUGGEST THAT ANY WIFE TAKE CARE of the checking account herself and leave her husband out of it. That way you can keep track of his spending and he will have no idea what you have been spending on yourself. Sell him the idea by telling him how busy he is already and how tedious bookkeeping can be. She who handles the checking account controls the money and the marriage.

—SHIRL MAWHINNEY
PORTERSVILLE, PENNSYLVANIA
💔 13Y

. . . .

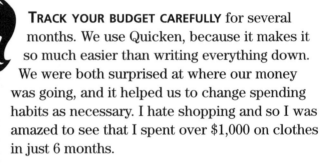

TRACK YOUR BUDGET CAREFULLY for several months. We use Quicken, because it makes it so much easier than writing everything down. We were both surprised at where our money was going, and it helped us to change spending habits as necessary. I hate shopping and so I was amazed to see that I spent over $1,000 on clothes in just 6 months.

—K.T.
BURLINGTON, VERMONT
💔 5Y

. . . .

MY HUSBAND AND I FIRMLY BELIEVE that purchasing a new home is a wonderful way to start earning a "nest egg." We bought our first home 11 months after we were married. Sure, it was hard to be house-poor for a while, but paying rent is difficult, too, and renting gives you nothing to show for the sacrifice of tough budgeting. Once you're in the game of real estate, you can surely parlay the money secured from the sale of that home into a much bigger, newer, or better-situated property.

—ANITA KEMPE
JACKSON, NEW JERSEY
💔 32Y

MONEY WAS A BIG ISSUE FOR US in the beginning. We fought about it all the time. I came from a very strong, responsible family. My dad was a financial director and he was very money-minded, penny-pinching. And I learned how to manage money and not be frivolous. On the other hand, my wife's father gave her everything she wanted and he never said no to her and she grew up with no respect for money at all and no idea how to manage it. This caused a lot of conflict in our marriage. She didn't understand why we didn't make much money in the beginning. We had to rent and we suffered through hard times. The good news is, we got through it, and I think that struggle has made our marriage stronger in the end.

—*BRIAN L. COY*
EL CAJON, CALIFORNIA
💔 25Y

● ● ● ● ● ● ● ●

" Figure out what amount in your checkbook will make you both sweat and twitch. Try to keep twice that on reserve. "

—*MARY M.*
SPRINGFIELD, ILLINOIS
💔 24Y

● ● ● ● ● ● ● ●

DON'T HIDE MONEY. Don't spend more money than you'd want your spouse to spend. And respect your money—it's your security and future.

—*SANDY*
WASHINGTON, DC
💔 3Y

DON'T MAKE BIG DECISIONS or purchases without consulting the other person.

—*S. COLEMAN*
NEW YORK, NEW YORK
4Y

• • • • • • • • •

YOU LEARN QUICKLY THAT THE PERSON who's best with numbers should handle the finances . . . and only one person should be in charge. At least that's been my experience. And I'm content to let my wife do it, even when it comes to negotiating the price of a new car. I once watched in awe as she reduced a grown Pontiac salesman to tears and managed to save us more than $5,000 in the process.

—*ANONYMOUS*
EL PASO, TEXAS
21Y

• • • • • • • • •

GIVE YOURSELF AN ALLOWANCE

Money used to be a huge source of conflict between my husband and I. I'm home with the kids, and he works. I was just going out with a credit card and buying whatever I wanted, whenever I felt like it. I was seriously spending about $3,000 a month just eating out and buying stuff for the house, and I wasn't even accountable for it. The way we dealt with this was to put me on a budget. Now, I get a set amount of money per month—$1,000— and if I go over that, I have to pick up odd jobs to supplement it. This system has really worked for our family—we don't have to discuss money anymore and it's allowed us to save a good deal. Some women might not like the idea of an allowance, but I look at it as my way of making a positive contribution to our family.

—*ROBYN MURAMOTO*
CENTENNIAL, COLORADO
19Y

I HIGHLY RECOMMEND USING A COMPUTER program like Quicken. I use it to keep all of our finances in line. It works as both a check register and budgeting tool. Plus, it creates charts and graphs so my husband and I can tell at a glance how much money and we have and how we're spending it.

—*ANONYMOUS*
BIGLERVILLE, PENNSYLVANIA
4Y

• • • • • • • •

UNLESS YOU ARE FABULOUSLY WEALTHY, agree that monthly expenses (including what you buy on credit!) will be less than monthly earnings. This sounds pretty obvious, but wait until the credit card debt begins to grow. It gets messy when it catches up with you. Beyond that, everyone should be free to spend how they please. Just keep it below the monthly income ceiling.

—*ROBERT*
ATLANTA, GEORGIA

• • • • • • • •

FINANCES SHOULD BE DONE TOGETHER. But, someone should take the lead role, preferably the person who is better at understanding money and how to organize it. That person should help his or her spouse learn how to be disciplined with money.

—*DREW*
SYRACUSE, NEW YORK
5Y

• • • • • • • •

YOU NEED TO SAVE MONEY to allow for emergencies: What if someone gets fired? What if someone gets sick? What if disaster strikes?

—*DAWN COLCLASURE-WILSON*
RANCHO MIRAGE, CALIFORNIA
2Y

MY HUSBAND IS VERY BAD AT CALCULATING TIPS.
I always have to make sure he's done the math
correctly and left the full 20 percent.

—*AMANDA*
ATLANTA, GEORGIA
2Y

* * * * * * * *

" Get yourself one of those big
5-gallon water jugs and throw
every coin you come into
contact with in it. It doesn't
seem like much at the time,
but when you get that sucker
filled and start rolling those
coins you will be amazed at
how much you've saved. It
beats using those two bits to
buy a candy bar. "

—*BRIAN HORZICH*
WHEELING, WEST VIRGINIA
6Y

* * * * * * * *

WE HAVE AN UNSPOKEN RULE that you can spend
up to $100 without checking with the other, but
beyond that, it is a discussion.

—*ALISON WEISS*
HALF MOON BAY, CALIFORNIA
17Y

TALK ABOUT FINANCES. From the very beginning of our marriage, my husband and I have spent every Thursday night paying bills and talking about our finances. This way, we both always know where all of our money is, and where it's being spent. We come up with strategies for saving and spending our money. We set goals, work together to achieve them, and then celebrate when we meet them.

—*JENNIFER BRIGHT REICH*
HELLERTOWN, PENNSYLVANIA
💔*1Y*

• • • • • • • •

YOU HAVE TO BE "ON THE SAME SHEET OF MUSIC" financially. My husband and I went to a financial planner right after we got married and made some concrete plans about our future. It worked very well. We've saved a lot of money for our future. Most importantly, we don't have to argue about money. That's freedom!

—*BETH*
OKLAHOMA
💔*16Y*

• • • • • • • •

Another reason to pay off your credit cards: Research shows that debt brought into marriage is the No. 1 problem area for newlyweds.

—*NEWLYWED DEBT*

GET INTO THE HABIT OF PUTTING MONEY into a Christmas club account each year. No matter how much you want to think you will have the money when you need it, you don't want to have to run up those charges. A little money put away in the summer will go a long way come the holidays.

—*DYLAN TOOMEY*
WHEELING, WEST VIRGINIA
💔*20Y*

MY WIFE AND I KEEP SEPARATE BANK ACCOUNTS, although we split all the expenses and have quite a bit of common property. We have always maintained a great degree of independence within our relationship and I think that our marriage is actually stronger for it. Though we have our responsibilities in the marriage, there remains much that we do for one another by choice rather than obligation. For example, with a separate bank account, the gifts I buy her are not being paid for from our pooled resources. It's me deciding on my own to spend my money on her.

We also very rarely argue about money, which I'm always hearing is the most common source of discord among couples. We both know, of course, that the other would help out in times of need. We've never had to do that on any large scale, but I know she would take care of me if I was out of work and she knows I would do the same for her.

—*T.B.*
ATLANTA, GEORGIA
2Y

Never bring up his or her earning potential. Especially in a derogatory way.

—*DOUG BRIMMER*
COLORADO SPRINGS, COLORADO
13Y

• • • • • • • •

BEFORE SPENDING OUR WEDDING MONEY, my husband and I made a list of the things we needed or wanted for each room. Then, we started watching the ads and buying stuff as it went on sale. This saves you a lot of money because you're not going out and buying things impulsively that you may not end up liking in the long run. We waited three whole months to get our bedroom set, which was worth it because we ended up with exactly what we wanted.

—*JAYME O'FALLON*
MISSOURI
4M

BUYING VS. RENTING

THE POSITIVE SIDE TO RENTING WHEN YOU'RE FIRST MARRIED is the money you save on home repairs. I didn't know a socket wrench from Uncle Sam, and I still don't, so I figured we could save a bunch of money by letting the landlord worry about anything that went wrong. If you buy a house, that's all on you.

—*KADESH HARDIE*
FROSTBURG, MARYLAND
4Y

• • • • • • • •

CONSIDER BUYING A HOUSE BEFORE you get married. My husband and I made sure that we had a house to move into when we got married, so we kind of had the house first. It made for a very exciting beginning!

—*DONNA*
ALLENTOWN, PENNSYLVANIA
13Y

• • • • • • • •

INSTEAD OF IMMEDIATELY BUYING A HOME you can't really afford, open a savings account and save money while earning interest over time. If you save, you'll have more money in the end.

—*J.L.P.*
DAVENPORT, IOWA
30Y

• • • • • • • •

IF YOU DON'T GET OFF TO A SOLID FINANCIAL START—like we didn't—buying really isn't an option. But we had so many people telling us what a waste of money renting was and how we were throwing our money away. But there was nothing we could do about it. No bank would have financed us. The upside was that I got to learn how to cook and ruin someone else's stove.

—*M.K.M.*
OWINGS, MARYLAND
1Y

IF YOU CAN AFFORD IT, a good and cheap invest-ment is savings bonds. My husband and I give savings bonds to all of our nieces and nephews for all their birthdays and Christmas. They don't earn tons of interest but they also don't mature for years so the kids can't waste the money and it will be there when they need it most—for college.

—*PAM SASSER*
WHEELING, WEST VIRGINIA
21Y

• • • • • • • •

GET PAPERWORK ORGANIZED. My husband and I used to argue because we would each be buying things, but the receipts would be all over the house and often lost. The solution was so simple. I bought a basket with a handle and hung it on the wall in our kitchen. We put all of our receipts in there. No more lost receipts!

—*KRISTEN*
BETHLEHEM, PENNSYLVANIA
9Y

• • • • • • • •

MY HUSBAND LIVES SO IN THE MOMENT, he has no financial plan. He'll go to Moab or Baja over pay-ing the electric bill.

—*SUSAN D.*
MISSOULA, MONTANA
7Y

• • • • • • • •

ABOUT THE ONLY SORE POINT WE HAVE with money is my lack of interest in the stock market. He thinks I should get very excited and make invest-ment decisions. I told him, "No problem! As soon as you get excited about meal planning then I'll share your enthusiasm for financial planning."

—*V.B.*
DOHA, QATAR
28Y

I HAVE A SINGLE FRIEND WHO ONCE ASKED me how much it cost me to be married. I said, "What do you mean?" And he said, "How much do *you* keep out of your salary?" I said, "It's shared. Whatever money I make goes into our family and whatever money she makes goes into our family. There's nothing I keep for myself." And he said, "Oh, because I'm single I get to keep it all." He admitted that he spent about $200-$300 a month on dating. But that was it. He said, "So it costs you everything to be married." That comment kind of set me back for a minute, until I realized that he was just being a little bit selfish. He couldn't share his money or his emotions totally with somebody. He couldn't understand that next step.

—*DUANE STONE*
MIAMI, FLORIDA
26Y

• • • • • • • •

WE GOT IN THE BIGGEST FIGHT in our marriage over one dollar. I was supposed to make a deposit of $51. But I was thirsty so I took the dollar and bought a Big Gulp. He told me he couldn't trust me with our money. It was the principle to him. But I said, "It was hot. I wanted a drink. What's a dollar?" We fought for three days over one dollar. I kid you not.

—*TINA M. COY*
EL CAJON, CALIFORNIA
25Y

Don't forget to count your blessings. When you're balancing your budget and counting your money (or lack thereof) you should also remember to count how many times you laughed together during the week.

—*CAROL UMMEL LINDQUIST, PH.D.*

WHEN WE WERE YOUNGER AND STARTING OUT, we really needed to save money. Also, we didn't want to just collect a bunch of stuff. So for our anniversaries, we decided we would not give each other presents; we would go out to a special meal together. That's what we've always done, and it's been fantastic.

—LORI T.
CHARLESTON, SOUTH CAROLINA
38Y

Spice of Life:
Sex and Romance

*W*hen you first met, you couldn't keep your hands off each
other. But as your marriage has evolved, most likely your
twice-a-day "appointments" with each other have tapered off to once
a week, once a month, once a . . . And what about romance?
Remember flowers? Remember phone calls to say, "I love you?" What
happened to that? Better read on. To keep a marriage working, you
need to keep spending alone time with your spouse, even—or maybe
especially—if there are kids in the picture. And you need to make
that time productive. Here's how.

WE HAVE TWO FAVORITE THINGS: We like to climb
into bed with candy and watch the Red Sox, and we
love to get in the car and drive endlessly and look
around the countryside. We just drive and explore.

—*MARSHA H. DONAHUE*
CAPE ELIZABETH, MAINE
♥1Y

**SEX GETS
BETTER, BUT
LESS FREQUENT.**

—*D.W.*
ATLANTA, GEORGIA
♥8Y

AHH, THE FIRST DATE: You picked her up, probably brought her flowers, and definitely opened every car and restaurant door in order to impress. After you get married, she's still that same girl who wants to be swept off her feet and be made to feel, if only for a moment, like someone's princess. Continue opening the doors. Oh yeah— and kiss a lot.

—*ANONYMOUS*
MINNEAPOLIS, MINNESOTA
5Y

. . . .

" **Display pictures of just the two of you. It reminds you (and everyone else) that there is strength and love that begins with that relationship.** "

—*M.L.M.*
SPRINGFIELD, ILLINOIS
20Y

. . . .

KEEP IT INTERESTING BY ALWAYS being attentive and giving. It can't just be all about you. You have to be concerned about the other person. You have to want to make them feel as good as you feel. Sometimes you have to give of yourself when there's no return. And if you truly love someone, you'll give of yourself without even thinking about it.

—*W.D.O.*
ATHENS, GEORGIA
4Y

MY FATHER TOLD ME THAT THE THINGS you do to get a woman are the things you do to keep her. If I bought my wife flowers every Thursday when we were dating, I buy her flowers every Thursday now that we're married. If we knocked boots three times a week before the wedding, we knock boots three times a week after the wedding as well. This is the best advice ever because it means that the best things about your relationship never change.

—*STEVEN GREEN*
LOS ANGELES, CALIFORNIA
💔*10Y*

Go to strip clubs. I buy my husband dances and I buy myself dances.

—*PILAR*
ATLANTA, GEORGIA
💔*4Y*

• • • • • • • •

YOU NEED TO MAKE SURE YOU HAVE SEX regularly. There's a connection between intimacy and spirituality. If you're not having good, regular, sweaty sex, I don't think you'll feel as connected to your partner. You need to touch each other a lot. You need to kiss a lot, even if it doesn't lead to something more serious. You've got to stay physically connected.

—*J.H.*
ATHENS, GEORGIA
💔*5Y*

• • • • • • • •

ALWAYS EXPECT YOUR PARTNER TO DESIRE more than you can offer. Don't fall into the trap of thinking you are the ultimate, because then you'll become arrogant and lazy. I am forever looking at guys who are better looking and better mannered than myself because it helps keep my attitude in check. After all these years, every time my wife and I have sex, I still try hard to please her.

—*EMMILLIO E.*
VANCOUVER, CANADA
💔*33Y*

AFTER YOU GET MARRIED, things will inevitably become less romantic—which is OK. But I let the relationship slip into a brother-sister vibe, which was not good at all because it zapped all of the sexuality out of everything. Do your best to keep things steamy, at least one night a week.

—MOLLY F.
NEW YORK, NEW YORK
5Y

• • • • • • • • •

BEING IN LOVE IS DIFFERENT THAN being married. Being married is a very real, in-your-face, some-times-good, sometimes-bad thing. And it doesn't have a whole lot to do with love. The most important thing is being best friends. It sounds cliché. But if I have a problem, there aren't other people that I call first. I call my wife. In some ways, marriage is like the best roommate situation you could ever have.

—ANONYMOUS
ATLANTA, GEORGIA
10Y

THE BIG LITTLE THINGS

We genuinely like each other, and we both go out of our way to show that we are thinking of each other and understand each other's love-language. My husband likes to be touched— back scratched, feet rubbed. I do this for him. He puts little notes in my lunch box and calls me every day just to talk. I air-dry his clothes on the clothesline. He makes sure that we have Diet Coke in the house. I never complain when he wants to play basketball on Sundays. He makes sure I have time to read mysteries in bed. After 17 years, it is the small things that will keep you connected.

—ALISON WEISS
HALF MOON BAY, CALIFORNIA
17Y

I KEEP THE ROMANCE ALIVE IN MY MARRIAGE by doing simple, unexpected things. A card in the mail or placed on the counter; a rose placed under the windshield wiper or delivered to work or home; a surprise dinner of favorite foods; and letting her know she is the most important person in the world to me.

—*R.A.*
CEDAR RAPIDS, IOWA
25Y

• • • • • • • •

BE AWARE OF SLEEP PATTERNS AND NEEDS. My fiancé needs about two to three more hours of sleep each night than I do. That's a drag since we love going to bed and waking up together. The compromise is a small desk at the foot of our bed where I keep my laptop. I wake at my usual hour and get to work—checking e-mails, writing stories, doing research, etc. We're still together, but I'm not lying in bed "wasting time" and he's not getting up crankily. When his alarm goes off, I crawl back in bed with him and we "wake up" together.

—*M.C.L.*
CHAPEL HILL, NORTH CAROLINA

• • • • • • • •

MY WIFE BRINGS ME FRESH FRUIT IN BED almost every morning. She gets up and peels an orange or slices an apple and brings it back to bed and feeds me. There's been no drop-off in that area since we got married.

—*J.C.*
WASHINGTON, DC
3Y

• • • • • • • •

BE GOOFY. Always keep a sense of humor.

—*GEOFF*
ANN ARBOR, MICHIGAN
2Y

"My wife met me at the door the other night in a sexy negligee. Unfortunately, she was just coming home."

—*RODNEY DANGERFIELD*

Dine by
candlelight.

—*ANONYMOUS*
  WASHINGTON, DC
  33Y

WHEN YOU MARRY A WOMAN her body will never look the same as it will look on your honeymoon. The moment she has her first baby it will change. You have to love them beyond the body.

—*TINA M. COY*
  EL CAJON, CALIFORNIA
  25Y

• • • • • • • •

IT'S OK FOR SEX TO BE THE THING that brings you together; that's just human biology. But it won't be the thing that keeps you together.

—*STEVE*
  HOLLYWOOD, CALIFORNIA

• • • • • • • •

AVOID THE TRAP OF FEELING that you have to spend loads of money or time to be romantic. Pluck a camellia from a neighbor's yard and present it to your wife one night. Put a love letter in his briefcase. My fiancé and I often leave little notes on the pillow or in the fridge for each other.

—*M.C.L.*
  CHAPEL HILL, NORTH CAROLINA

• • • • • • • •

LEARN TO BE CREATIVE AND ADVENTUROUS. Routine is the end of a good sex life. You need to add spice, whether that means trying new positions, locations or toys. Make a trip to a sex store with your partner and just walk around and look at stuff. They have every kind of sex toy imaginable there. You probably won't know what to do with half of them, but that's OK, because their sales people are all about excellent customer service!

—*TIM GETZOFF*
  BOULDER, COLORADO
  5Y

SET A "CLOSED DOOR" RULE. In our home, doors are always open—unless there's a good reason for them to be closed. We feel this is important for privacy and respect. We close our doors when we are changing clothes, of course, but my husband and I even sleep with our bedroom door open. If we need privacy for intimacy, we close the door. Our girls know that if that they need us, they may knock on the door, but they may not open it. This gives us the privacy we need.

—*TORI DENNIS*
IRON CITY, TENNESSEE
 *10Y*

* * * * * * * *

" You know what they say about marriage: Sticks and stones can break my bones, but whips and chains excite me. "

—*ANONYMOUS*
GEORGETOWN, GRAND CAYMAN
23Y

* * * * * * * *

SEX IS PRETTY DARN NEAR THE TOP of the list of importance in marriage. I can cook my own food, wash my clothes, mow the lawn, and feed the dog. But taking care of that kind of business is best handled with a partner. Being married to my best friend, instead of the person I was passionate about, led to less than satisfying sex. I believe, though I can't prove it, that that was the missing link in our marriage.

—*ROBERT*
ATLANTA, GEORGIA

YOU DID WHAT? SHARING YOUR SEXUAL PAST

THERE IS NO ROOM FOR SECRETS IN A MARRIAGE. Since we had both been married before, we each had a lot of history. My mate wasn't looking for an unsullied virgin. Experience has turned out to be a good thing, since we've both enjoyed the sexual techniques each has learned from the past.

—*JOANNE SPROTT*
HOUSTON, TEXAS
2Y

• • • • • • • • •

SOMETIMES, YOU JUST HAVE TO WHITEWASH YOUR HISTORY a little. There's a very real possibility where I live of running into two of my serious exes. We don't talk about those guys much, because my husband is just really jealous of them. But overall, I actually like being able to mention and share our pasts.

—*ANNE B.*
SAN FRANCISCO, CALIFORNIA
2Y

• • • • • • • • •

HE DIDN'T LIKE IT MUCH AND IT CAUSED A FEW FIGHTS in the early pre- and post-wedding days. As far as I could tell, there was no benefit to telling him anything. His imagination just went wild.

—*ANASTASIA M. ASHMAN*
ISTANBUL, TURKEY
3Y

• • • • • • •

MY HUSBAND AND I WERE BOTH VIRGINS until our wedding night. We couldn't have done it any other way and had it be as special an experience.

—*WHITNEY JASINSKI*
RENTON, WASHINGTON
3Y

YEAH, I WOULD HAVE LIKED TO HAVE HAD MORE EXPERIENCES. But I'd rather lose 20 pounds.

> —*L.K.*
> *CHARLESTON, SOUTH CAROLINA*
> 21Y

· · · · · · · · ·

SEXUAL SKELETONS ARE THE HARDEST TO TALK ABOUT. But once they're out, the relationship will be stronger. You'll earn trust. Do you want your spouse to find out about something about your past after you've been married for five years? How much you share, however, depends on your spouse's comfort level. You have to be careful. You can't just dump all your skeletons on someone in one sitting. Do it slowly over time.

> —*W.O.*
> *SYRACUSE, NEW YORK*
> 9Y

· · · · · · · · ·

WE DIDN'T MEET WHEN WE WERE TWO YEARS OLD. We met when we were adults. So, she had things in her past that I'm not particularly crazy about, and vice versa. But we forget that because we've got bigger things that we've created together.

> —*KEITH*
> *ATLANTA, GEORGIA*
> 4Y

· · · · · · · · ·

WE SHARED EVERYTHING. I think that's important. My spouse knows almost more about me than I do. And vise versa. He was fine with it. And I was fine with his past.

> —*EMBER NEVILL*
> *FT. WORTH, TEXAS*
> 2Y

THERE'S ALWAYS THAT ONE GUY YOU IDEALIZE, and even when you're married, you think to yourself, "I'd give it all up for him." Of course you wouldn't, but it's still totally natural to have that fantasy.

—JEN W.
SAN CARLOS, CALIFORNIA
26Y

• • • • • • • •

SEX IS MUCH LESS FREQUENT NOW that we're married. I'm not really surprised about it. I actually expected it. Sex has never been the most important part of my marriage. There are just many other issues that we're managing now such as work, our son, money, personal time, etc. Yes, I would like to have sex more frequently with my wife, but I'm satisfied with our sex life right now. In marriage, I learned that everything is a cycle. So, I expect that we'll be back in full swing soon. I'm looking forward to it!

—J.K.
SWEDEN
7Y

• • • • • • • •

MEN SHOULD UNDERSTAND THAT WOMEN NEED sex just as much as men do, though they might not communicate it. I think women still have a problem expressing their needs and instead they'll subjugate it and it will show in various forms of frustration in their daily lives. Men should offer sex on a regular basis and not be upset if she doesn't accept it because she still has to deal with a lot of things that we don't even understand.

—DOUG FINCH
BRATTLEBORO, VERMONT
TWICE

AT SOME POINT, YOU PROBABLY WILL NOT want to have sex every night. Work, life and routine will conspire against your libido (usually). But that doesn't mean you have to sacrifice your sex lives. Wear sexy underwear, don't go to bed in ratty jammies and be sensual and intimate whenever you can. A healthy sexual relationship is so much more than nightly coitus.

—*M.C.L.*
CHAPEL HILL, NORTH CAROLINA

• • • • • • • •

MEN, YOU STILL NEED TO MAKE YOUR WIFE feel desired and sexy. Now more than ever is the time to make sure you compliment her on how sexy she looks or catch her by surprise and kiss her in the middle of her sentence, leave her a love note in her jacket pocket. Don't ever stop doing things like that. You will never know how important that "little" stuff is to her. Women, don't take it personally if he's not jumping your bones every night. You'll need to work at it, too. If you are used to him initiating all the time, then switch it up. Surprise him by greeting him when he comes home from work in a sexy piece of lingerie. Make yourself irresistible. And sometimes you'll have to tell him what you want . . .

—*JEN*
CASTRO VALLEY, CALIFORNIA
5M

Chores, school and work get in the way of a happy marriage. The Center recommends that spouses connect with each other in small ways—a gesture, a loving word, a card, developing a ritual of 'us' time.

—*CENTER FOR MARRIAGE AND FAMILY STUDIES*

DON'T PLAY THE VIDEO GAME EVERYDAY. It might get boring. Keep it new and try playing the game in different rooms, at different angles, with different obstacles.

> —*RICHARD HALL*
> *KENNESAW, GEORGIA*
> ❤️ *10Y*

• • • • • • • •

"My wife and I started a treasure chest of love letters when we were engaged. Now, on every anniversary, we go away and take the stack of love letters with us. We spend at least three days traveling to some place we've never been and review all the passionate moments that we've had over the years."

> —*MARK JAPPE*
> *SANTEE, CALIFORNIA*
> ❤️ *21Y*

• • • • • • • •

HE WANTS SEX *TO* FEEL CLOSE. I want sex *when* I feel close.

> —*SAM*
> *ATLANTA, GEORGIA*
> ❤️ *3M*

WHEN THE KIDS WERE YOUNGER and we wanted to have fun in the bedroom, we'd set up the kids in front of the TV and we would go upstairs. It would be like we were teenagers again, sneaking around. And we would do our thing and go downstairs and they would still be sitting there watching their show. It was great. But I think it's harder to be intimate in your own house as the children get older. They know what's going on. My daughter knows we're not going to bed at 7 p.m. You come out of your bedroom and you act like you're doing something wrong. It's uncomfortable. I have to wait until they're not home or asleep.

—*TINA M. COY*
EL CAJON, CALIFORNIA
25Y

* * * * * * * *

I WISH WE HAD MORE SEX. Everything else is great. We have affection and tenderness, but not enough sex. I think maybe we have different "styles" of seduction and just don't have the energy very often to overcome that. We both are perplexed by this.

—*R.*
AUSTIN, TEXAS
3Y

* * * * * * * *

MAKE TIME FOR EACH OTHER, and as cliché as this may sound, remember that this relationship is more important than even the parent-child relationship. The kids will grow up and leave and you and your spouse will be back alone as a couple. It's too late to work on things if at that point you realize you have nothing in common and have ignored the relationship all these years.

—*ALISON*
BOCA RATON, FLORIDA
8Y

He still brings me flowers on the 25th of every month, because that is the date we got engaged and got married.

—*L.M.*
NEW YORK,
NEW YORK
3Y

SEX IS NOT AS IMPORTANT AS SPENDING quality time and experiencing life together. Try to stay physical with your spouse, but realize there is more to life than sex.

—SANDY
WASHINGTON, DC
3Y

• • • • • • • •

I 'VE ALWAYS THOUGHT THAT SEX IS IMPORTANT. But it has become a tricky thing these past couple years. It takes me a lot longer to get in the mood nowadays. I don't think it's the curse of marriage. I'm assuming it could just be due to stress. Whatever the cause, I'm not as "hot to go" as I used to be. Of course, my husband is *always* hot to go. I know that it's important that I make the effort to stay in touch with my sexuality, not just for my own fulfillment, but for my relationship with my husband, too. I still think he's incredibly sexy and I love him more now than I ever have.

—S.
BOCA RATON, FLORIDA
2Y

• • • • • • • •

JUST REMEMBER THAT YOU CAN HAVE great sex with anyone. But you can only have the total package with one person.

—G.
ANN ARBOR, MICHIGAN
2Y

• • • • • • • •

MY HUSBAND AND I WATCH PORN. It gets us going. Every time we go to a hotel, we check to make sure they have those adult movies. Then we take care of the rest.

—SARAH
ATLANTA, GEORGIA
6Y

When on a date with your spouse, stay positive. This is not the time to tell your mate what he or she has done wrong in the past ten years.

—LOVEGEVITY.COM

MEN, READ THIS . . .

ALWAYS PRETEND THAT EVERYTHING YOUR WIFE is wearing is new, even though you have seen it 30 times before. It makes her feel good.

> —*BILL W.*
> *SEATTLE, WASHINGTON*
> 33Y

WASHING DISHES AND DOING LAUNDRY IS FOREPLAY. Forget about going out and buying dinner. It's the housework that counts—especially if you're the one that works and your wife stays at home with the kids. Do you want that hot vixen you first fell for? Do the dishes. Vacuum. The next morning, cook her breakfast. Leave her a note telling her how beautiful she is. Call her from work and tell her how you can't stop thinking about her. Cook dinner. Put the kids to bed early. Draw her a bath. Then light some candles. Put on some soft music. Help her dry off, lead her to the bedroom. The payoff will be great.

> —*ANONYMOUS*
> *SYRACUSE, NEW YORK*
> 5Y

WHEN THE SEX STARTS GOING DOWNHILL, you know you're in trouble. My wife and I were still sleeping together, but the emotional connection wasn't there any longer. All of the sudden, she was saying things like, "Let's just get this over with!" Having sex felt more like a chore than something she wanted to do.

> —*JOHN*
> *GREELEY, COLORADO*
> 24Y

Once a day, kiss for at least seven seconds!

—*K.R.*
NEW YORK,
NEW YORK
7M

MY GRANDMA AND GRANDPA have been married 60 years. Her advice is to keep the romance alive. One year ago the cover story of *Time* magazine was entitled, "Sexless Marriages in America." My grandma was appalled and said sex keeps it going—sex, romance and intimacy.

> —*TALLIE FISHBURNE*
> *MINNEAPOLIS, MINNESOTA*
> *5Y*

* * * * * * * *

I'VE HAD TO LEARN NOT TO COMMUNICATE desires, wants, likes and dislikes in bed, unless I say it in a sexual way, like: "Hey, baby, I've been thinking about X all night long." Otherwise, I bring up problems/ideas when we're alone and it's quiet— and when he's in a good mood.

> —*COURTNEY ALFORD-POMEROY*
> *ATHENS, GEORGIA*
> *1Y*

* * * * * * * *

ROMANCE DOESN'T HAVE TO DIE after the wedding. My husband planned a surprise trip to Paris for me last year, after 13 years of marriage. It was the most exciting trip I've ever been on. The fact that he thought of it on his own, tried to surprise me, made arrangements for child care and took me to one of the most historically romantic places in the world still gives me a lump in my throat.

> —*ANONYMOUS*
> *PETALUMA, CALIFORNIA*
> *14Y*

THE RUSH OF SEXUAL ATTRACTION AND DESIRE does not last. In good marriages it is replaced by mutual respect, compromise and a deep abiding love that is nurtured every day.

—*NANCY*
TAMPA, FLORIDA
22Y, ,

• • • • • • • •

WE TRY TO DO NICE, UNEXPECTED THINGS for each other at times. I think I'm most impressed by seeing my husband all dressed up, when he smells nice, when we're out alone, and I feel like we're on a date again.

—*ANONYMOUS*
LOS ANGELES, CALIFORNIA
11Y

• • • • • • • •

" Men, don't pressure women about sex. Women, understand where the man's brain actually is. Everything will work out. "

—*KERRI SACKLYN*
MARIETTA, GEORGIA
6Y

• • • • • • • •

WE GO OUT TO DINNER AND SPEND TIME TOGETHER. And when we're alone, he washes my hair for me. He's even styled it for me. Women appreciate that. When a guy does simple things like that, girls really love it. He draws my bath for me and gets the bubbles ready. And I'll do things like that for him.

—*M.C.W.*
WESLEY CHAPEL, FLORIDA
* TWICE, 2Y*

ON GIVING . . .

DO NOT MISS ANNIVERSARIES. Don't even think about it. I have never missed an anniversary. We don't do anything big. But we go out to dinner.

> —*ANONYMOUS*
> *BETHESDA, MARYLAND*
> 💔, 💔 *12Y*

WOMEN DON'T REALLY WANT CANDY OR FLOWERS. They want jewelry.

> —*S.C.*
> *HELOTES, TEXAS*
> 💙 *31Y*

IF YOU'RE GIVING YOUR PARTNER A BIRTHDAY PRESENT, make sure that one of the things you give demonstrates that you actually listen and know what she or he wants. Be perceptive and observant and demonstrate that you care about the little things.

> —*J.H.*
> *ATHENS, GEORGIA*
> 💙 *5Y*

WE SURPRISE EACH OTHER ON OUR BIRTHDAYS EVERY YEAR. We never know what the other has up their sleeves. Once, I arranged overnight childcare for our youngest son and took my husband out for his birthday. He didn't have a clue what he was in for. First, I took him to a spa for a hot tub and massage; then I led him to a favorite restaurant, where we gorged on special dishes and desserts; then I whisked him away to the city, to see a symphony and finally kept him overnight at a bed and breakfast, where we made love until the sun shined through the lace curtains.

> —*A.*
> *CHICAGO, ILLINOIS*
> 💙 *18Y*

I WAS DUE WITH OUR FIRST CHILD ON MAY 15. I wanted a Mother's Day gift from my husband, and he said, "Only if you're a mother." Well, the baby was born very early, on April Fool's Day. So, not only was I a mother, but after six weeks, I was feeling pretty much back to normal. I expected some beautiful gift, maybe something sexy. What I got was a diaper bag and an umbrella. I realized then that I hadn't married the most romantic guy. But the diaper bag did come in handy.

—*BONNIE DULFON*
BOSTON, MASSACHUSETTS
💔*45Y*

• • • • • • • • •

FOR OUR FIRST ANNIVERSARY, MY HUSBAND BOUGHT ME AN APRON. I was horrified, shocked and angry, because I assumed he was subliminally saying I needed to stay at home like a 1950s housewife. He kept assuring me that wasn't true, but it led to a big fight anyway. Fortunately, this fight evolved into a long talk about our expectations and desires. I learned he was sort of old school because he wanted nurturing. At the same time, he respected me more because I went to school, worked and made money, which made me feel a lot better. I also learned not to assume there's hidden meaning behind every gift. Sometimes, guys will give unusual gifts because they really think you want them. He was truly shocked to see how angry the apron made me.

—*PAMELA BARTH*
BAKERSFIELD, CALIFORNIA
💔*25Y*

SOMETIMES WE'RE TOGETHER SO MUCH I feel like he must take me for granted. But then he'll do or say something that makes me realize that he really loves and understands me.

—*R.*
AUSTIN, TEXAS
3Y

• • • • • • • •

"For a fun, budget getaway, we have 'Tim & Kate's Bed & Breakfast.' We don't answer the phone or watch TV and no one is allowed to contact us for that weekend. We treat it like a vacation at home. We go out to eat for every meal, see plays and go hiking as if we were tourists in our own town."

—*KATE MOYNIHAN*
MINNEAPOLIS, MINNESOTA
5Y

• • • • • • • •

I GET UPSET THAT WE NEVER GO on real dates and that he's not a creative romantic.

—*ANONYMOUS*
ATLANTA, GEORGIA
1Y

DO NOT UNDERESTIMATE ATTRACTION. Make sure everything else important is there but do not discount this component. When I have not seen my spouse in a while and he returns, I am always struck by how attractive he is. This is a pleasure that adds much to our marriage.

—*JENNIFER B.*
YARDLEY, PENNSYLVANIA
5Y

• • • • • • • •

FROM MY FIRST MARRIAGE I found out that, contrary to what John Lennon said, love is *not* all you need. Sometimes love dries up, or disappears, or changes. You need plenty of other things in addition to love, such as attraction, common interests, respect, and patience.

—*JENNIFER G.*
ROCK HILL, SOUTH CAROLINA
4Y

• • • • • • • •

I THINK SURPRISES ARE GREAT TO KEEP romance alive. One year I kidnapped my husband for our anniversary! I told him that we were going away, but I didn't tell him where. He had always wanted to stay overnight in Atlantic City, NJ. So I packed both of our suitcases and some special treats like champagne while he was at work, and then I picked him up at the end of the day. I made up convoluted directions, pretending that our destination was half an hour past Atlantic City. But at the last minute, just before we drove past the hotel, I said, "Turn here." He was so surprised, especially when he saw the suitcases!

—*MOLLY BROWN*
ALLENTOWN, PENNSYLVANIA
23Y

In a marriage, you have to have a good sex life. Seriously!

—*MARGARET*
BELLEVUE,
WASHINGTON
35Y

THE THINGS SPOUSES DO . . .

LET ME SLEEP IN. I think this happened once. I guess buying me a big diamond was pretty nice, too.

> —*D.W.*
> *ATLANTA, GEORGIA*
> 8Y

• • • • • • • •

THE NICEST THING I EVER DID FOR MY SPOUSE was surprise him with a cruise for our anniversary. I packed his bag and called his boss. He thought he was going to work and I took him to the airport instead.

> —*KERRI SACKLYN*
> *MARIETTA, GEORGIA*
> 6Y

• • • • • • • •

HE DOES NICE THINGS FOR ME EVERY DAY: makes me coffee, calls me at work, cooks me dinner, cleans the cat box. He's so supportive in whatever I want to do.

> —*SHANNON*
> *BOCA RATON, FLORIDA*
> 2Y

• • • • • • • •

THE NICEST THING MY WIFE HAS EVER DONE FOR ME was give me three healthy boys. With marriage and careers, there is a realization that time is valuable and whenever possible the family comes first. I always spent time with my wife and boys when they were younger, and now it's great to visit and talk to them. We've developed strong relationships with each of them.

> —*J.L.P.*
> *DAVENPORT, IOWA*
> 30Y

• • • • • • • •

I'VE SHOWERED MY WIFE WITH LOVE AND AFFECTION, sired her two children, and bought her a vacuum with a headlight.

> —*B.P.*
> *ORLANDO, FLORIDA*
> 3Y

SOMETIMES, YOU NEED A CHANGE OF SCENERY for romance. And it's something you have to plan. We don't have spontaneous romance. We were able to get away about a year ago to do some hiking in North Carolina, but we had to plan for three weeks just to get a few days away. We had a fabulous time, but it wasn't easy getting there. And when we're away, we have one rule: No talk about the kids. To enjoy romance, I think you have to revert to the time when you didn't have kids.

> —*JANE*
> *BROOKLYN, NEW YORK*
> 20Y

• • • • • • • •

TO ME, ROMANCE IS NOT ABOUT FLOWERS. I don't like candy or the typical candlelight dinner. That doesn't do a thing for me. I'm always like, "Can we turn on the light so we can see what we're eating?" Try cooking a meal in the nude and, uh, eating it on the coffee table in the living room. It has to be a different place. It's not what props you use, it's how you feel. You have to find a place where you feel uninhibited. When we were younger, it was just about sex. We didn't have to be romantic, we had energy. Now it's about more than that.

> —*CATHY WESTMORELAND*
> *CHURCHVILLE, VIRGINIA*
> 20Y

• • • • • • • •

WE GO ON REALLY NICE VACATIONS. We have two weeks of time-shares in St. Martin and go every year. We have a few drinks and relax and we get into conversations that we never have when we are home. Sometimes I make him tell me things that he likes about me, and vice versa. It's our time to "rediscover" our relationship.

> —*SHARI SUGARMAN*
> *NORTH BABYLON, NEW YORK*
> 13Y

"Figure out how sex got moved down the priority list," says Dr. Phil. "One of the biggest mistakes that couples make is when they have children, they stop being friends and lovers . . . Being a parent is just one of the roles that you play, and neglecting the role of partner and lover is a huge mistake."

—*O MAGAZINE*

So many men don't have a clue what women really want—like a single rose for no reason. That's one of the things I love most about my husband.

—*BARBARA STEVENS*
GATLINBURG,
TENNESSEE
💟 *26Y*

TRAVEL LIKE COLLEGE STUDENTS. Put backpacks on and go somewhere like you have no responsibilities. We packed only what we could fit into our backpacks, got on a plane and spent a month in Thailand. We felt like we were 18 again.

—*TOM FISHBURNE*
MINNEAPOLIS, MINNESOTA
💟 *5Y*

• • • • • • • •

WE HAVE LITTLE NICKNAMES FOR EACH OTHER. Most of them are in Spanish. I'm from Mexico and I call him *"tortuga"* and *"chaparrito."* We don't have English names at all. I say them and he repeats them and I laugh. Instead of calling me *"chaparitta,"* which is the feminine form, he calls me in the masculine form. And then he calls me *"mi vida,"* which means "my life."

—*BARBARA*
PUEBLA, MEXICO
💟 *9M*

Balancing Act: Making Time for Work *and* Play

O*ne of the hardest parts of marriage is learning how not to collapse in front of the TV at the end of a long day at the office, then go to sleep. You're married now, and your partner (and kids) need you to carve out time for them, too. One of the most important things you can do for your family is find ways to make yourself available to them on nights and weekends, and when you're in the office, too. How can you balance all those balls without dropping them? Read on.*

WE HAVE DINNER TOGETHER EVERY NIGHT. A lot of families are on the go and they never sit down. But I think it's important to have that regular, set time to be together as a family.

—*K.J.*
ST. AUGUSTINE, FLORIDA
9Y

ALL HUSBANDS SHOULD BE REQUIRED TO GO AWAY NOW AND THEN.

—*B. MILLS*
HILLSBORO, OREGON
31Y

MY WIFE AND I HAVE A FAVORITE MOVIE: "Jaws." We watch it at least once a year, and we've even pulled our "marriage motto" out of it. There's one scene where Police Chief Brody is chumming the waters and griping about his duties . . . when all of the sudden, Jaws himself pops up, huge and frightening, and nearly bites Brody's head off. This is the first real sighting of the huge shark by Brody, and he is trembling with fear as he slowly walks back to Quint, the salty captain. With a cigarette dangling from his dry mouth, Brody says, "We're gonna need a bigger boat." Marriage—and life in general, really—is like that. Something's always popping up that disrupts the daily routine. Financial trouble, career trouble, challenges with the kids, and on the lighter side, great vacations, funny moments, financial gains.

—*JWAIII*
   ATLANTA, GEORGIA
   9Y

. . . .

TALK ON THE PHONE at least 5 times every day.

—*M.S.*
   TORONTO, CANADA
   14Y

. . . .

EVERY DAY IS CRAZY, IN A GOOD WAY. We don't plan anything. We don't plan vacations. We don't buy tickets two weeks in advance because we don't know what we might want to do the next day. Every day we live with surprises. Every day is excitement. Every day we are waiting for the morning to see what it will bring.

—*ALEEZA CALLNER*
   LOS ANGELES, CALIFORNIA
   10Y, ; 22Y

I THINK THE KEY TO HAVING YOUR CAKE and eating it too—having a career and keeping a happy family—is energy. It can be exhausting to work all day and then come home to make dinner, clean the house and still have quality time with the kids. You can only do it if you feel good. I know it got a lot easier for me once I decided to start taking better care of myself and eat better. I know it sounds cliché, but it really works. You don't realize how much energy you are missing out on until you get it back.

—MARCY CHILDS
FROSTBURG, MARYLAND
2Y

If you are a stay-at-home mom, set the table for dinner before your husband comes home from work. That way he'll think you know what you're fixing, even if you don't.

—LEE MONTOPOLI
RIVER DALE, NEW JERSEY
6Y

I'D REALLY LIKE A RELATIONSHIP INTERN. My husband and I are often too, uh, lazy to get our dry cleaning, prepare meals, etc. and we often joke about hiring a relationship intern to do all of our errands. In turn, we'd teach them the secrets of maintaining a successful relationship.

—AMANDA
ATLANTA, GEORGIA
2Y

A SUPER COUPLE

HIS: **FUN TRADITIONS ARE IMPORTANT IN A MARRIAGE.** My wife and I used to bet each year on the Super Bowl. One of our daughters would be on my team, and the other daughter would be on my wife's team. The night of the game, we'd have a special dinner of treats, such as cheese fondue, stuffed mushrooms, and shrimp cocktail. Then we'd all watch the game together. The winning team got to pick a restaurant to go for a special dinner. One year, my wife picked the restaurant inside Cinderella Castle at Walt Disney World. We live in Pennsylvania, so this wasn't *exactly* within the rules. I didn't argue, though. I wanted to go, too!

> —JOHN R. BRIGHT
> ALLENTOWN, PENNSYLVANIA
> 💔35Y

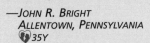

HERS: **IT'S GREAT TO HAVE TRADITIONS IN YOUR MARRIAGE** and in your family. In my case, our tradition paid off in a really unexpected way. Each year, my husband and I bet on who would win the Super Bowl. The winner usually got to choose the location for a special dinner out, but one year we bet that whoever lost would have to do the dishes for two straight weeks. My team won that year, and before my husband's two weeks of dishwashing were over, I had a new dishwasher!

> —MARY
> ALLENTOWN, PENNSYLVANIA
> 💔35Y

WHAT I LOVE MOST ABOUT MY HUSBAND is also what annoys me the most: his ambition. He is a workaholic. The benefit is that he makes a lot of money and is well respected in his career, and he is not always hanging around the house. The hardest part is that he isn't around much to help with the kids. I accept my husband's work ethic but require that he help by giving the children their baths and playing with them for a short time after work. I also demand that when he is at home, his mind must be at home, too. I require no less than 110 percent!

—*LORRAINE BRANCATTO BOERSMA*
TOLEDO, OHIO
♥ 8Y

. . . .

THE SECRET TO A GOOD MARRIAGE IS to take business trips—to have some time apart, just because you're always so happy to see each other again. It worked for us. Especially when we were young, we just couldn't wait to be together.

—*JACK MORRIS*
WALTHAM, MASSACHUSETTS
♥ 45Y

. . . .

I THINK MY JOB HAS SOMETHING TO DO WITH the fact that I've been married for so long. My job takes me away for a week at a time and I think that helps in my marriage. I don't know how people do it day in and day out, going home every night. When we're together, we spend all our time together and it's great.

—*DUANE STONE*
MIAMI, FLORIDA
♥ 26Y

For a perfect marriage: Have a cleaning lady, separate bathrooms and order groceries online.

—*L.M.*
  NEW YORK,
  NEW YORK
  3Y

START A BUSINESS: My husband retired a few years ago. Going from 40 peaceful hours at home by myself to 40 hours of "togetherness" made me nuts. So I started my own part-time business with my best friend, creating flower arrangements. We work two days a week—at her house, not mine. It's probably saved my marriage—it's definitely saved my sanity!

—*MARY BRIGHT*
  ALLENTOWN, PENNSYLVANIA
  35Y

* * * * * * * *

EVERY COUPLE MUST SPEND TIME TOGETHER on a regular basis. My husband and I each lead very full lives. But we often spend time together to experience what the other is doing. For example, I have attended every one of my husband's softball games. In turn, my husband comes to my volunteer and church events. These simple activities give recognition and importance to our marriage.

—*PAT Q.T.*
  CALIFORNIA
  35Y

* * * * * * * *

WE HAVE ISSUES ABOUT HAVING "ALONE" TIME at home to get work done. He gets very grumpy when he thinks I'm disturbing his creative genius. And now we argue over which of us will watch the baby so the other one can work. We vent our frustration by blowing up at each other. Then when that's out, we can more calmly discuss what each of us is unhappy about and negotiate a solution. Our most productive solutions are often preceded by a nasty argument. It's like we prod each other into blowing up and losing our tempers, and then we can have a good, productive discussion.

—*ANONYMOUS*
  AUSTIN, TEXAS
  3Y

TALK WITH YOUR WIFE THROUGHOUT THE DAY. Just because you're at work doesn't mean you're off limits. My wife and I are constantly calling each other to arrange plans and deal with our six kids. She will call me to say our son is either going to get a ride with a kid we don't know or I have to pick him up and drive him to the movie theater. If she didn't call me to try and work it out, I wouldn't have the option to say, "Sure, I'll figure out a way to pick him up later."

—V.P.
MUNDELEIN, ILLINOIS
23Y

· · · · · · · ·

I KNEW IF I WANTED TO EVER SEE my new husband, I needed to learn how to play golf. So I did. He tried to teach me, but you learn better from someone else. Once we started playing, I found out that it doesn't really matter how many shots you take on a hole, as long as you walk fast so as not to hold up the people behind you.

—D.J.
SOUTH RIDING, VIRGINIA
5Y

· · · · · · · ·

HAVE A SENSE OF HUMOR IN MARRIAGE. Laugh at yourself. I remember when I first met my husband I was very uptight, very serious. I took everything to heart. Every time someone critiqued me, I would really get hurt by it. He taught me that life is too short not to just laugh and live. Just have a good time. My husband would be like, "Who cares if there's dirt on the floor? It's more important to spend time together and talk to your kids."

—LISA
CHARLOTTE, NORTH CAROLINA
3Y

A COUPLE THAT COOKS TOGETHER . . .

COOK TOGETHER! I can't stress enough how close this can bring you with your husband. Before we were married, mine didn't even know how to cut a carrot or boil a pot of water. When you cook together, it makes you enjoy what you're eating even more and it never feels like a chore.

> —STACI KESSLER
> HIGHLAND PARK, ILLINOIS
> 8Y

ALWAYS HAVE DINNER TOGETHER WITH THE TV OFF. It's a great time to bond and talk about your day.

> —RENAE
> ATLANTA, GEORGIA
> 3Y

MY HUSBAND SAID EARLY ON THAT HE WAS ALWAYS going to tell the truth about things like how I looked or food I made so that when he said, "Great!" I'd know he really meant it. So one time, I'd made some tomato-rice dish for dinner. He looked up from eating it and said, "This tastes like ass!" We still laugh about that all the time.

> —KATRINA CURRIER
> SAN FRANCISCO, CALIFORNIA
> 3Y

I THINK IT'S SUCH A TREAT WHEN SPOUSES COOK for each other. In my 35-year marriage, I've done almost all of the cooking. But in later years, now that my husband's retired, he makes lunch for me almost every day. Usually it's just sandwiches, but it means so much to me.

> —MARY
> ALLENTOWN, PENNSYLVANIA
> 35Y

DETERMINE WHO LIKES TO COOK AND WHO DOESN'T LIKE TO COOK.
And if you both don't like to cook, live in a place where you can order takeout easily. My husband and I are both horrible cooks. But we really love to eat out.

—*TRACY*
ATLANTA, GEORGIA
4Y

. . . .

WATCH THOSE COOKING SHOWS ON TV WITH YOUR WIFE. It makes you both interested in what's for dinner and it's easier to plan together when you have someone on the screen telling you what to do.

—*D.R.*
EVANSTON, ILLINOIS
6Y

. . . .

MY HUSBAND PRETTY MUCH INSISTS THAT HE CLEANS UP when I cook. What's really wonderful is that he also cleans up when HE cooks!

—*CHRISTINE BEIDEL*
RUTHERFORD, NEW JERSEY
3Y

. . . .

WHOEVER IS HOME AROUND DINNERTIME SHOULD COOK. The woman shouldn't just be expected to whip up a meal because that's what people think wives should do. Share the work and expect that the person who has time to plan a meal does so. If you're both working and too busy to cook, then go out for a bite.

—*STEVE*
BUFFALO GROVE, ILLINOIS
14Y

LEARN TO BE FLEXIBLE AND OPEN to different ways of living. In the 35 years we've been married, we've moved to 17 countries! We've had a completely different family life than I ever would have imagined. We've had such great experiences together. And our house could be a museum!

—*PAT Q.T.*
CALIFORNIA
🎔 35Y

• • • • • • • •

" You should do what's best for you as a couple to achieve your long-term goals. That might mean that each of your careers, from time to time, has to take a backseat. "

—*ANONYMOUS*
CARLTON, GEORGIA
🎔 4Y

• • • • • • • •

MY HUSBAND HAS A MISTRESS: HIS JOB! He is as dedicated to his job as he is to our marriage! While that is sometimes very nice because he makes good money, it is also pretty annoying because we never spend time together. It used to be very difficult accepting his work ethic. Now, I realize that when I'm OK with myself, then I'm OK with him—and his mistress.

—*F.T.L.*
METZ, FRANCE
🎔 7Y

JUST A PHONE CALL TO SAY HI from work each day can go a long way. Everyone wants to know that they are loved.

—*JIM RODDY*
PITTSBURGH, PENNSYLVANIA
20Y

. . . .

TO SUCCESSFULLY BALANCE CAREER AND FAMILY life, don't ever let work come first. I'm an editor at a newspaper and when I started my family, I told my bosses point blank that football games, concerts and birthdays for my kids come first. If you don't get that out of the way, the timing will never be appropriate. And if you work in a place that doesn't value your family, maybe you should get a different job.

—*SARAH HANSEN*
CHICAGO, ILLINOIS
11Y

. . . .

ABOUT SEVEN YEARS AGO, I was working at a software company. We were testing a piece of software, and my wife provided a bug report, by e-mail. One of my colleagues noticed that she e-mailed it to me at our house, while we were both home. This was something of a novelty then. Now we use e-mail and text messaging a lot. I don't like to talk on the telephone and don't like to be interrupted, and e-mail and text messaging allow you to respond on your schedule.

—*T.B.*
SOUTH PORTLAND, MAINE
10Y

NEVER STOP DATING YOUR HUSBAND OR WIFE. Just because you are settling down in a marriage doesn't mean the fun and excitement has to settle down. Pick a night during the week where instead of coming home from work and watching TV, you go to a different restaurant or see a movie or meet at a store and pick out something for your place. The earlier you fall into a boring routine, the earlier you get bored with each other.

—*AMY HOFFMANN*
EVANSTON, ILLINOIS
💕 *8Y*

• • • • • • • •

MY HUSBAND AND I HAVE BEEN MARRIED for 35 years. But a few years ago, we discovered a hobby that might surprise you: X-Box! We play video games together, and now we have X-Box Live so we can play against people from all over the world. It might seem unusual, but in just the past few months I've met quite a few other couples our age who share the same hobby.

—*ANONYMOUS*
LONG VALLEY, NEW JERSEY
💕 *35Y*

• • • • • • • •

MY WIFE AND I LIKE TO DRINK TOGETHER. Drinking facilitates conversation and that's true with your spouse as well. When you drink together, you talk. The more you drink, the more you get to know a person. You never run out of things to say.

—*ANDREW*
KNOXVILLE, TENNESSEE
💕 *10Y*

THE MOODY PART OF MARRIAGE

GET SOME DISTANCE WHEN YOUR SPOUSE IS HAVING a mood swing. When my wife is having a mood swing, I focus on something else, even if that means moving to a different room in the house. This way I don't feed into her bad mood.

> —JON
> BIGLERVILLE, PENNSYLVANIA
> 3Y

• • • • • • • •

GO EASY ON YOUR WIFE DURING "THAT TIME OF THE MONTH."
When I have PMS, I get emotional. I cry. Sometimes it lasts for a week. My husband says everything he does for that week is wrong. But sometimes to me it feels like during that week he needles me even more.

> —ANONYMOUS
> LONG BRANCH, NEW JERSEY
> 2Y

• • • • • • • •

MOOD SWINGS: JUST ACCEPT THAT WE ALL HAVE THEM. Get out of the way and don't react to them. If you start in on each other you're just making things uglier. Learn to recognize when he's having one and then purposefully ignore it. It will pass and things will go back to normal.

> —BRETTE SEMBER
> CLARENCE, NEW YORK
> 15Y

• • • • • • • •

WHEN YOUR SPOUSE IS HAVING A MOOD SWING, it's a good idea to have an understanding friend. When my husband is in a mood, I go to my best friend's house and hang out there for a while.

> —ANONYMOUS
> ALLENTOWN, PENNSYLVANIA
> 35Y

WE SUPPORT EACH OTHER'S ENDEAVORS, even if they don't always seem the best route to take. We are two very different people now than we were when we first married, but we have each adapted to our new selves and take everything in stride. We live a very unstructured life because we know better than to expect that life will go according to some pre-planned itinerary. We are rigidly flexible.

—*TERI*
SYLVANIA, OHIO
29Y

. . . .

MY HUSBAND WAS AWAY FOR THREE WEEKS out of every month for business so we had to work at staying connected. How did we do it? He would call me 2 or 3 times every day. I learned early on that I didn't want to spend those phone calls on mundane details that I could handle myself. I wanted to know what my husband was doing and tell him what I was doing and how I was feeling. Those phone calls were (and still are) our connection to each other.

—*VIRGINIA T.*
CHICAGO, ILLINOIS
37Y

. . . .

I NEVER ASK MY HUSBAND, "When are you coming home?" He works hard and often late into the night. But I let him know that I appreciate his hard work and that he supports us by giving him the space he needs for his work. I expect the same from him.

—*WENDY*
MIAMI, FLORIDA
8M

IT'S IMPORTANT TO MAKE COMPROMISES when technology allows work to intrude on your family. I have a very demanding job and need to be available by phone to answer questions and handle issues. My wife gets upset, though, when calls interrupt our family time. So we agreed that I don't take work calls while we're eating dinner, or even right before we sit down to dinner.

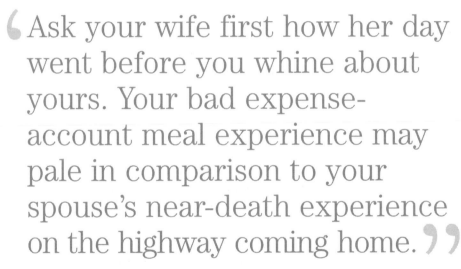

—*JON*
BIGLERVILLE, PENNSYLVANIA
3Y

• • • • • • • •

“ Ask your wife first how her day went before you whine about yours. Your bad expense-account meal experience may pale in comparison to your spouse's near-death experience on the highway coming home. ”

—*J.W.*
LAKE OSWEGO, OREGON
31Y

• • • • • • • •

IF MY WIFE AND I WANT TO WATCH different shows at the same time, she usually watches the TV in our living room, and I watch the one in our bedroom.

—*JOHN R. BRIGHT*
ALLENTOWN, PENNSYLVANIA
35Y

PEOPLE GET INTO A RUT. You have to change something in yourself to get out of it. When this happened to me, I did a lot of yoga, which made me realize that I was solely responsible for my own happiness.

—MEL MOLINO
MILL VALLEY, CALIFORNIA
💔20Y

• • • • • • • •

EVEN IN A HOME WITH A STAY-AT-HOME mom who does most of the cooking, you can help balance things out by having a weekly pancake tradition with Dad cooking. Or French toast. Or waffles. Whatever. And once your kids are old enough, let them take over! Our kids have experimented with some weird flavors (marshmallow pancakes come to mind), but we all enjoy the tradition.

—M.S.
NEW YORK, NEW YORK
💔20Y

• • • • • • • •

I ENCOURAGE PEOPLE TO ONLY HAVE ONE TV. That way you can't sit in separate rooms each watching your own show. I think that just having one TV encourages communication and compromise, even if it's on a small level. TV watching isn't an issue in our house. We simply watch TV together as a family.

—ANONYMOUS
BIGLERVILLE, PENNSYLVANIA
💔3Y

MY SPOUSE RESPECTS THE FACT that I sometimes need space to be alone, to do things for myself and that I sometimes need to travel and see new things alone, or with a friend.

—*ANONYMOUS*
BOSTON, MASSACHUSETTS
2Y

* * * * * * * *

IN THE SUMMER, OR DURING SOME SCHOOL holidays when we're home, I take my kids to their Dad's office and let them go out to a nice lunch. Meanwhile, I run errands, read a book, or enjoy some time alone. It has become a really special tradition and time for them together. Also, it helps my husband keep that home/work balance he wants.

—*K. JONES*
PHILADELPHIA, PENNSYLVANIA
15Y

* * * * * * * * *

MY WIFE'S E-MAILS ARE WHAT GET ME THROUGH the hours at work. She gives me updates on what our daughters are doing and reminds me that she loves me. What could be better? It's an e-mail so no one else notices besides me. If it was phone calls all day at the office, it wouldn't work.

—*STEVE*
BUFFALO GROVE, ILLINOIS
14Y

* * * * * * * *

MAKE SURE YOUR SPOUSE KNOWS every day that they are important to you. You can only control your own behavior. You can't change the way people feel and what they do. But you can affect your behavior to help them know that they are the person for you.

—*PAT WILLIAMS*
ATLANTA, GEORGIA
13Y, ; 8Y,

Entertainment: We played board games into the wee hours of the night because it was inexpensive.

—*JANICE*
CINCINNATI, OHIO
35Y

A COUPLE THAT SWEATS TOGETHER . . .

I NEVER THOUGHT IT WOULD BE SOMETHING I'D LIKE DOING with my husband, but when we go to the gym together it's actually fun. You have someone to talk to on the treadmill or cardio machine. There's someone to spot for you when you're lifting weights. It's also a bonding activity for the two of you—something more to talk about at home.

> —SUSAN
> GLENVIEW, ILLINOIS
> 13Y

DO EXERCISE INDIVIDUALLY. We used to try to do exercise together and it just never worked because he goes faster and works harder than I do, and if he goes at my pace he says it isn't a workout. We do try to do some things together like playing tennis and taking walks in the woods, but we don't rely on those activities for our exercise.

> —BRETTE SEMBER
> CLARENCE, NEW YORK
> 15Y

WHEN I GO TO THE GYM, IT'S MY OWN THING. I encourage my husband to do it when it's convenient for him, but I like going by myself and taking my time there. I hate going with him because I feel rushed when I want to stay longer than him. Men work out quickly and women shouldn't be afraid to just take their time.

> —STACI KESSLER
> HIGHLAND PARK, ILLINOIS
> 8Y

I VOTE FOR EXERCISING TOGETHER. My husband and I go for a 30- to 45-minute walk almost every day with our dog. We have a favorite two-mile route that we follow most days, to keep it simple. Besides the great health and weight loss benefits, our walks are special times for us. Many of our best talks have been on walks. We talk about serious things sometimes, mundane things other times, but our best walks are when we're in silly moods and we just laugh and laugh as we walk.

> —*JENNIFER BRIGHT REICH*
> *HELLERTOWN, PENNSYLVANIA*
> 1Y

* * * * * * * *

IT'S SIMPLE: HEAVY WEIGHTS AND BENCH PRESSING are for men and yoga classes and pilates are for women.

> —*CAROLINE SMITH*
> *EVANSTON, ILLINOIS*
> 12Y

* * * * * * * *

I'VE BEEN A RUNNER FOR YEARS AND HAVE COMPETED in several marathons and many shorter races over the years. My husband doesn't run, but he's always supportive when I'm training for an event. He also comes along to the races to cheer me on, and supplies me with water, snacks and massages afterwards. He used to lift weights so he understands the "buzz" I get from a good run. In fact, when I'm cranky, he's been known to suggest that maybe I need a run!

> —*KELLY JAMES-ENGER*
> *DOWNERS GROVE, ILLINOIS*
> 7Y

ONE THING THAT HAS REALLY HELPED ease the strain, and by extension helped our marriage, was to have our daughter help out around the house as much as possible. She does laundry, sets the table and clears the dishes, feeds the pets, and takes out the garbage. With her help around the house, the long hours my husband is away are less burdensome.

—*SANDI LLOYD*
ALLENTOWN, PENNSYLVANIA
17Y

• • • • • • • •

GO OUT TO BREAKFAST A LOT. We take the kids out to breakfast almost every weekend. Because we can't often eat dinner together during the week, these weekend breakfasts have become really important. Plus, when you spend time together on Saturday or Sunday mornings, you don't have to talk about homework!

—*E.T.*
PORTLAND, MAINE
18Y

• • • • • • • •

LEARN HOW TO COOK A FEW SIMPLE but elegant foods. My family sits down at the table together most nights, and at least a few nights a week we find ourselves marveling at how fantastic our dinner is, even though we got it on the table quickly. We might start cooking at 6:45, and by 7:15 we're eating grilled pork with chutney, couscous salad, and steamed beans with a butter-lemon sauce. Yum!

—*MISSY*
DETROIT, MICHIGAN
18Y

MAKE ENOUGH FOR 10 EVEN THOUGH there are only a few of you. If it's freezable, freeze it in smaller portions for great leftovers on a day you don't feel like cooking. If it's something that can be transformed—like plain chicken into chicken salad—use it for another meal. This way, you don't spend all your time cooking.

> —*DENISE*
> *BOSTON, MASSACHUSETTS*
> 7Y

• • • • • • • •

I'M A STAY-AT-HOME MOM, but I try to meet with my husband once a week for lunch. We found a playground by his office, and we just grab quick sandwiches and let our daughter play on the play-ground with her Daddy (and Mommy). Also, he gets to show her off to everybody in the office.

> —*CHRISTINE B.*
> *NEW YORK, NEW YORK*
> 1Y

• • • • • • • •

MY HUSBAND HAS A VERY STRESSFUL, demanding job in IT where he's putting out fires all day. Often he comes home overloaded and/or exhausted. I used to pester him about what was wrong to try to get him to "talk about it" so he'd feel better, but that usually made mat-ters worse. Over the years, I've learned to ask, "How are you doing? Do you want to talk about anything? Or would you rather be left alone?" If it's the latter, I give him his space, and after a couple of hours, his "mood" has usually worn off.

> —*KELLY JAMES-ENGER*
> *DOWNERS GROVE, ILLINOIS*
> 7Y

WE E-MAIL EACH OTHER SEVERAL TIMES throughout the day, and it helps to keep us connected even though we are each doing our own thing. I find e-mail to be useful in place of a "to do" list. We also find cell phones useful for when we're out shopping. He usually goes off with our son and I'm usually with our daughter, and we use cell phones to plan where to meet up.

—BRETTE SEMBER
CLARENCE, NEW YORK
15Y

The Daily Grind: Pet Peeves and House Rules

*H*e leaves his dirty socks on the floor. She never remembers to take the garbage out in the morning. You can't agree whose turn it is to walk the dog, or who gets to control the remote. These things are going to come up every day for the rest of your married lives. Our advice: figure out early on what bugs you about your beloved, and find ways to cope—make house rules, chore lists, and practice taking deep breaths when those inevitable pet peeves peek out at you from every nook and cranny.

WE DIVIDE THE CHORES UP VERY SIMPLY: She does everything that requires skill and detail, and I do everything that requires a light once-over or heavy lifting.

> —*ALLAN JAFFE*
> *PETALUMA, CALIFORNIA*
> 13Y

IT'S A FREE FOR ALL!

> —*E.T.*
> *PORTLAND, MAINE*
> 18Y

MY HUSBAND AND I ALWAYS TRY TO LOOK at the big picture and the long term. Dirty socks on the floor every night can be annoying, but in the relative scope of things, love and companionship, common dreams, and shared values are what matter most.

—CATHY
NEW YORK, NEW YORK
❤️ 10Y

• • • • • • • •

❝She hates it when I use the last of the toilet paper and don't replace the roll. But I notice that she doesn't use the whole roll. She leaves just a little bit left so that I'm the one who has to change it.❞

—GREG JANTZ
PONCA CITY, OKLAHOMA
❤️ 7Y

• • • • • • • •

DON'T EVER KEEP COUNT. Phrases like, "I've done the dishes three nights in a row, now it's your turn" or "The last seven times we've gone out to eat, you've chosen the restaurant" have no place in a healthy marriage.

—ANTHONY MANUEL
KINDER, LOUISIANA
❤️ 14Y

IN THE BEGINNING, SIT DOWN AND MAKE A LIST of all the chores that need to be done, then divide them equally. DON'T just assume the woman will be doing everything. Marriage is a partnership and the work should be divided equally. My husband takes care of the yard and house maintenance, the grocery shopping and the bill paying, because those are the things he is good at. I do everything else. This system has worked well for us. We still use it to this day.

—*CHERI HURD*
LITTLETON, COLORADO
32Y

. . . .

TAKE TURNS WITH THE CHORES. Don't just divide up the stuff that needs doing around the house and then constantly do the same stuff over and over. That gets incredibly monotonous. One week it's your turn to do the dishes or take out the garbage, and the next week you do the laundry and load the dishwasher. Variety is the spice of life.

—*BOB SCHULTZ*
HOPEWELL, PENNSYLVANIA
3Y

. . . .

WE BOTH WORK FULL-TIME. It's really hard for both of us to maintain a clean house all week, so we use Saturday mornings to get everything really clean. Usually, we're done in an hour or so and can move on. I've learned that my husband doesn't initiate doing chores but is willing to help if I give him a specific assignment. So, I never have to worry about taking out the trash, and he never has to worry about having clean clothes. It's all give and take, so if he doesn't help around the house, then he has to take me shopping.

—*WHITNEY JASINSKI*
RENTON, WASHINGTON
3Y

I have become a more flexible person since being married. At first, I couldn't even touch my toes; now I can vacuum, dust, and cook.

—*B.P.*
ORLANDO, FLORIDA
3Y

Are you losing? Do you even know what you might be losing? Women keep score in a marriage. They allocate one point per action or gift. Most men, are clueless to this point-scoring system.

—Barbara and
  Allan Pease

SOMETIMES THE BEST WAY TO CREATE a life together is by making do with less. If you have only one car between the two of you, then you'll spend more time together because you can't take separate vehicles everywhere you go. If you never buy a television, you'll spend more time playing games and talking to each other. In fact, not having a television is a wonderful way to get rid of all the false expectations found in dramas, commercials, and "reality" television.

—Bridgette R.
  Lansing, Michigan
  12Y

. . . .

I ADMIT, I AM AN ANAL PERSON, but when you first get married you have to sit down and divvy up the chores. It's so easy to come home from work and just want to chill out on your new couch and watch your new TV. You have all these new "toys" that you got for your wedding and shower presents to play with. Before you know it you'll be living in a pigsty.

—Angela
  Frostburg, Maryland
  6Y

. . . .

ACCEPT THAT HE HAS A DIFFERENT WAY of doing things. Hold your tongue and think twice before you let that little barb go because you will regret it later. It's just stupid little things, like the fact that while I cook and he cleans up, he puts my cutting boards in the dishwasher. You have to let things go and choose your battles, otherwise you spend your life fighting over the smallest things. The only exception is the toilet seat—men can be trained to put it down. I'm working on my sons now.

—J.V.
  Randolph, Vermont
  14Y

PET PEEVES

SHE LIKES THINGS A CERTAIN WAY—the house for instance. Aspects of our daily lives that I don't really think about, she puts a lot of thought and energy into. She can't sit down to do anything else until the laundry is folded and put away, whereas if I have an idea or something I want to jot down, or if I just want to sit and do nothing, I'll do it. We frustrate the hell out of each other this way.

> —JAMES
> FRANKFURT, GERMANY
> 5Y

ONE OF MY PET PEEVES IS HIS "STUFF" on the kitchen counter—mail, wallet, cell phone, keys, PDA, briefcase, etc. Plus he's a horizontal space hog. He's incapable of stacking things on top of one another, so the kitchen counter is always strewn with his stuff. He spreads stuff out. I stack it up, move it to his office, and throw stuff out, whatever. Finally, I asked him if he would mind if I left my dirty pots and pans and other kitchen tools on his desk. It took him a moment, but he got the message.

> —JAN ALDER
> ATLANTA, GEORGIA
> 7Y

HE'S VERY NAGGY ABOUT OUR HOUSE, especially when he's stressed, and it drives me crazy! Also, he's tidy and I'm clean. In other words, he's fine as long as things look tidy, and I don't mind untidy as long as things are clean. This causes a lot of household tension. He smacks his gum and chews like a cow. Often he gets into his own head and spaces out and forgets to do little things like open the door for me, etc. He can be very grumpy.

> —ANONYMOUS
> AUSTIN, TEXAS
> 3Y

IT'S SO SILLY FOR HUSBANDS AND WIVES to stick to set roles. We're not living in the 1950s. I found this newspaper picture from when my parents first got married and did a promotion for a department store—my mom had her hair up in a beehive and was pouring coffee for my dad. The caption read: "Arlene Goldstein pours coffee for husband. Other hot beverages may be served in these large urns." I find that ad so hilarious because it's so completely different from how my parents' relationship really is. There were never any roles in my family. Both of my parents worked full-time and although my mom made dinner every night, my dad did all the ironing. I've never seen my mother "serve" my father. There are so many two-income families today, that there isn't enough time for specified roles.

—AMANDA
ATLANTA, GEORGIA
2Y

• • • • • • • •

I LIKE MY MUSIC LOUD AND SHE DOESN'T. She turns it down and I turn it off. If I can't hear it loud I don't want to hear it at all.

—ARMAND
SAN DIEGO, CALIFORNIA
5Y

• • • • • • • •

SWITCH DOING THE CHORES! I pay the bills, but my husband does a lot of the cooking. Then we'll switch chores—I'll cook and he'll pay the bills. We don't plan to switch; it just happens naturally. But neither of us feels unappreciated. And we both know how to manage the household chores.

—L.C.
PITTSBURGH, PENNSYLVANIA
12Y

MY WIFE AND I ALTERNATE WEEKS WE COOK. One week, I do all the grocery shopping and cook the meals and the next week she does it. If one person is doing all the work in a marriage it creates resentment and means there's something you *could* be sharing and aren't. We also make a point to sit down most nights and eat dinner with a glass of wine and candles. This means that every night we actually have a conversation. The cooking has also given us both an intensive interest in food, which is something else we share.

—*J.R.*
IOWA CITY, IOWA
18Y

● ● ● ● ● ● ● ●

WHEN WE HAD OUR FIRST KID, we wanted to stop swearing, so we set up a two-jar system: When somebody swore, they put $1 in their own jar. Once we got up to a sizeable amount, the person who'd sworn the least got to take all the money and do something fun for themselves. My wife got herself a massage. We would have kept going, but by then we'd managed to curb the habit, for the most part.

—*JERRY B.*
NEW YORK, NEW YORK
5Y

● ● ● ● ● ● ● ●

MY HUSBAND CALLS CLEANING, LAUNDRY, ETC., "mommy work." He shouldn't have to do "mommy work." I became the "mommy." One problem—we don't have any kids. He is not my child! He runs a town, but finds it difficult to put his socks in the hamper! This is an argument we have over and over, but you can't let these sorts of arguments carry over into the rest of your relationship.

—*M.*
LONG BRANCH, NEW JERSEY
2Y

I still have not seen the manual with "set roles" for a marriage.

—*L.M.*
NEW YORK, NEW YORK
3Y

WHEN IT COMES TO CHORES, specialize. I vacuum and do most dishes. My wife folds the laundry and cooks most dinners. I do the finances. She writes the thank you notes. That way, each person does what they do best or like best, and there's a lot less arguing about "whose turn is it?"

—*TONY T.*
SAN FRANCISCO, CALIFORNIA
4Y

• • • • • • • •

TRY TO EAT BOTH BREAKFAST AND DINNER with your mate. Even if it involves changing your work hours, just do it. This allows you to sit down, communicate, spend time and pay attention to one another.

—*J.M.D.*
NEW YORK, NEW YORK
5Y

• • • • • • • •

THE HOUSEHOLD RULE THAT MY WIFE AND I have is no TV in the bedroom. The bedroom is only for sleeping and "other things."

—*ANONYMOUS*
FT. WORTH, TEXAS
26Y

• • • • • • • •

TELL YOUR SPOUSE WHEN SOMETHING he or she does bugs you—in a nice way. My husband insists on leaving the dishwashing brush on the counter. It's not a big deal, but it bugs me because I want it to be put away in the drainer under the sink, WHERE IT BELONGS. Instead of letting that pet peeve fester until it turns into a MONSTER DEAL, I remind him. Bless his heart, he tries. Likewise, he reminds me that he likes to have his shirts hung up when they come out of the dryer.

—*L.A.*
IOWA CITY, IOWA
17Y

WE HAVE A SHOES-OFF POLICY IN OUR HOUSE to keep snow and mud off the floors, but sometimes you just forget one little thing and it's not worth taking them off and putting them on. So we cheat. But we've made it a policy that if the other person catches you, you're the one who has to do the vacuuming the next time. One time my wife heard me coming and tried to do a handstand in the middle of the hall so that I wouldn't "catch" her with her shoes on. She's not very good at handstands, though.

—*PAUL W.*
MINNEAPOLIS, MINNESOTA
3Y

. . . .

" Try not to lock your keys in your car while it's running. I did this at the mall one time. My husband has never let me forget it. "

—*AMY*
CHICAGO, ILLINOIS
7Y

. . . .

I FEEL LIKE I DO EVERYTHING AT HOME, but I try not to be resentful. My husband works really hard, and I have to remember that what he's doing will benefit us all. I have to remind myself he's not working weekends and late for the fun of it. It helps that I'm OK by myself. I like alone time.

—*K.C.*
SAN FRANCISCO, CALIFORNIA
4Y

I'M A LITTLE STRANGE. I'll admit that up front. However, I have to have the first sip of any of my drinks. This is not debatable. I have no idea why, but it's a house rule and was even part of our wedding vows.

—*BRUCE WARREN*
MILWAUKEE, WISCONSIN
💔 3Y

• • • • • • • •

I HAD TO LEARN TO NOT KEEP AN ONGOING LIST of who did more around the house because, undoubtedly, I always did more. It took me a while to learn that housework is not a competition; it's just life and it has to get done. If he's not keeping score, I shouldn't either.

—*JILLIAN LEWIS*
BROOKLYN, NEW YORK
💔 18M

• • • • • • • •

I HAVE TO ADMIT, I STRUGGLED a lot with traditional gender roles early in our marriage. I didn't want to be the housekeeper, grocery shopper, and present buyer. In the beginning of our marriage, my husband and I did a lot of these chores together, but as the years went on we started to slip into traditional gender roles. Surprisingly, I didn't get upset by this. By that time, we were so busy that it just made sense for us to do the chores that we were naturally good at. For example, I am good at grocery shopping because I watch our money more carefully than my husband does. If it was up to him, he'd stop at 7-11 all the time and pay 3 times as much. For me, the division of chores became not a gender issue, but a time management issue.

—*JENNY*
DENTON, TEXAS
💔 12Y

THERE'S ONE THING MY HUSBAND WILL NOT DO: clean the cats' litter box. So I respect that. And there's one thing I will not do: take out the garbage. So my husband takes care of that job all of the time.

—*ANNMARIE PEARSON*
GIG HARBOR, WASHINGTON
12Y

* * * * * * * *

IT'S OUR HOUSE RULE THAT THE PERSON who finishes the roll of toilet paper must get out the new roll and put it on the holder. Sometimes we're so childish about it, we'll rip off half-squares just to leave something on the roll. It's irritating, but in a funny way: It's just hard not to laugh when you've stranded your wife on the toilet with a microscopic sliver of paper.

—*J.W.*
ROCHESTER, NEW YORK
14Y

* * * * * * * *

MY RULES ARE SIMPLE: Whoever dirties it cleans it. A simple life is a happy life.

—*ERICA GRAHAM*
ACCIDENT, MARYLAND
3Y

* * * * * * * *

LOTS OF PEOPLE COMPLAIN that they don't have enough time to be together, but then when they are together, they watch TV. We bought an armoire to hide the TV, which really does wonders for keeping us—and especially the kids—from watching it mindlessly. We play board games and card games and have long, leisurely meals together.

—*TONY*
CHICAGO, ILLINOIS
19Y

The first few months we were married we fought, then I learned to pick up after him; we've been fine ever since.

—*CAROL*
BEL AIR,
MARYLAND
43Y

REMOTE ENVY

LADIES, JUST FACE IT: The man is in control of the remote. But if you are like me, you'll avoid fights by watching shows such as "While You Were Out" on The Learning Channel. Yeah, it's a show for women about decorating, but there's also the element of surprise in the show that men can relate to.

—ANDREW
EVANSTON, ILLINOIS
1Y

FIND WHAT SHOWS YOU BOTH LIKE TO WATCH and put the clicker on the coffee table.

—CHRISTIAN
MONTCLAIR, NEW JERSEY
5Y

WE DON'T SHARE THE REMOTE. It is his.

—D.N.
TAMPA, FLORIDA
25Y

WHO CARES ABOUT REMOTES? Get another TV! Besides, sedentary activities should be limited!

—*ANONYMOUS*
TAMPA, FLORIDA
24Y

. . . .

I'M A COMPULSIVE MUTER and I'm lucky that my wife allows me to control the clicker at all times.

—*GEOFF*
ANN ARBOR, MICHIGAN
2Y

. . . .

SHARING THE REMOTE AND DECIDING WHAT WE'RE WATCHING on the tube is a huge point of contention between me and husband. I like "The World's Craziest Police Chases" while my husband prefers "Charlie Rose." There is no sharing of the clicker in this family, only prying it out of tight fingers . . . and we refuse to get another TV because we want to watch together. Luckily, my husband doesn't watch sports and doesn't mind watching Jerry Springer as long as we're holding hands.

—*AMANDA*
ATLANTA, GEORGIA
2Y

. . . .

HOW WE DEAL WITH THE TV CLICKER? Turn off the TV and take a walk.

—*ANONYMOUS*
WASHINGTON, DC
33Y

I USED TO THINK YOU COULD HAVE a 50-50 marriage. And it just isn't true. I do 99 percent of housework. I've just accepted that this isn't fair or equitable, but I get a payoff in other ways. There are other parts of our marriage where he gives 99 percent. We also have 2 kids. If I insisted on his "fair" share, a lot of his free time would be spent doing chores instead of being with the kids.

—*ALISON WEISS*
HALF MOON BAY, CALIFORNIA
💔17Y

• • • • • • • •

YOU HAVE TO IGNORE THE ANNOYING things your spouse does. My wife always picks at things around the house and nothing is ever in the right place. I can't stand it, but I have learned to ignore it for the sake of not fighting.

—*COREY*
IOWA CITY, IOWA
💔2Y

• • • • • • • •

WHOEVER IS THE MESSIER PERSON really has to make an effort to clean up. In our case, that's me. I tend to leave things out once I've used them, and I don't mind that. But I have realized that it actually makes my husband stressed out and uncomfortable to have clutter and mess. So I've learned to make my messes when he's gone for the day or on a business trip and clean up before he gets home. In fact, when he's gone, I really let loose and it looks like a tornado hit the place! I see that as one of the perks of having the house to myself.

—*S. COLEMAN*
NEW YORK, NEW YORK
💔4Y

SPLITTING RESPONSIBILITIES 50-50 DOESN'T WORK,
I don't think. One needs to take the lead in any
responsibility and the other needs to offer help.
Finances, we don't talk about. I just handle them
all. I also cook all the time. So that takes it out of
the equation. My wife is the primary childcare
and healthcare worrier. But I also offer some support and guidance. Everyone is different in this.
You've got to find what works. But if the check
bounces, the food is burned and the kids are in
the hospital, you've got to make a change.

—BILL
BOSTON, MASSACHUSETTS
9Y

· · · · · · · ·

DON'T LET LITTLE THINGS CAUSE STRESS. Early in our
marriage, I made a big deal over things that were
really no big deal. For example, my husband's
parents would announce that they wanted to come
to visit. Inevitably, they would call at the last
minute and say they had decided to come a day or
two earlier than planned. I would get upset
because the house wasn't ready, grocery shopping
wasn't done, etc. Looking back, I should have just
let it roll off my back. I was anxious to impress
them with a clean house and good food. But it
didn't really matter.

—ANONYMOUS
KENNESAW, GEORGIA
8Y

· · · · · · · ·

IF IT BUGS YOU THAT YOUR SPOUSE squeezes
the toothpaste in the middle or doesn't put
the top on, get two tubes of toothpaste: one
for you and one for him.

—JAN ALDER
ATLANTA, GEORGIA
7Y

My husband
cleans the
bathtub. You
know how I
trained him?
He was in the
shower and I
handed him
some Ajax and
said, "Why
don't you
scrub it down
while you're in
there?" He's
been doing it
ever since.

—TINA M. COY
EL CAJON,
CALIFORNIA
25Y

WE-MAIL?

E-MAIL IS PRIVATE. No password sharing!

> —*ANONYMOUS*
> *TAMPA, FLORIDA*
> 24Y

• • • • • • • •

WE HAD TO GET TWO COMPUTERS because my spouse is obsessed with his e-mail.

> —*R.A.*
> *AUSTIN, TEXAS*
> 3Y

• • • • • • • •

YOU SHOULD EACH HAVE YOUR OWN COMPUTER AND E-MAIL accounts. It's not about stealth, it's just more practical. And if you're suspicious enough of your spouse to even CONSIDER reading his/her e-mail, you've got bigger problems than sharing hardware.

> —*M.C.L.*
> *CHAPEL HILL, NORTH CAROLINA*

• • • • • • • •

GET TWO COMPUTERS AND A WIRELESS NETWORK so you can IM each other.

> —*D.W.*
> *ATLANTA, GEORGIA*
> 8Y

• • • • • • • •

HAVE YOUR OWN E-MAIL, but trust that if your spouse reads everything there is nothing to hide.

> —*SANDY*
> *WASHINGTON, DC*
> 3Y

MY HUSBAND TAKES SUCH AN INTEREST in our home. On Saturday, it's time to get up and get busy around the house. He takes one end, and I take the other. He can do it all. No matter what your spouse is good at, though, the house chores need to be shared. If you can afford a house-keeper, then, by golly, pitch your money in there and do it. But if you can't, and you are both living there and both using dishes and using the towels—it should be a joint effort. My time is just as valuable as his. Set that as an attitude before bad habits start. It should be understood from Day One.

> —*BECKY PAVLIS*
> *KNOXVILLE, TENNESSEE*
> 1Y

. . . .

HOUSEWORK IS NOT SO MUCH A SOURCE of tension as a source of squabbles. We both like having our house clean and we both work together on the housework, but my wife's tolerance for clutter is much lower than mine. I like having a healthy amount of clutter so the house doesn't seem overly sterile while she likes everything to be in its place at all times. The result is, I like to say, that we both do the same amount of cleaning, except Barbara does it sooner.

> —*M. JUDE ORTIZ*
> *DALLAS, TEXAS*
> 2Y

. . . .

IF YOUR WIFE SAYS, "I LOVE YOU," say, "I love you, too." Don't say, "I know you do."

> —*ANONYMOUS*
> *CINCINNATI, OHIO*
> 3Y

The Tide's against them: Men do 29% of laundry each week, according to one study. But only 7% of women trust their husbands to do it correctly.

—*WWW.EXPAGE.COM*

Clean up the hairs after you shave. This drives them crazy.

—*Tom Harris*
Waynesboro,
Virginia
💔5Y

HE'S MESSY: NINE CUPS OF COFFEE OUT OF TEN, he spills. And when he makes a sandwich, he leaves crumbs on the counter. It makes me crazy. I feel like I'm chasing after a two-year-old. But I try to wait and bring it up later, when I'm not mad. And I try to keep it in perspective because he does all these other wonderful things. Last week, he left jam on the counter, then set the phone book on top. Of course, it stuck to the counter. I waited a day, then gave him a kind reminder.

—*Anonymous*
Columbia, Maryland
💔2Y

• • • • • • • •

RESPECT EACH OTHER'S PERSONALITIES. My husband and I are very different: He's outgoing and vivacious while I'm quiet and reserved. Sometimes, it's hard because I don't want a lot of people around or he doesn't want to be alone. But we learn to trade off—sometimes we lead a very public life and other times we lead a very private life. Knowing that this is the cycle makes the difficult times easier.

—*J.S.H.*
Houston, Texas
💔18Y

• • • • • • • •

I'M THE BUS DRIVER AND SHE'S THE PASSENGER. Many times she tells the bus driver where we need to go, but for the most part I'm a planner, and she's not. However, I couldn't tell you the style of home we have, the square footage, when the recycling goes out, who has dentist appointments, when the bug guy comes, how much our insurance costs, how to refinance our home. She is definitely the house manager.

—*Richard Hall*
Kennesaw, Georgia
💔10Y

BATHROOM DIPLOMACY

SOMEHOW THE BATHROOM SEEMS TO BE THE PLACE where you have to be prepared to make the most compromises. Here are two biggies: 1) Toilet seat goes down. End of discussion. 2) Get separate tubes of toothpaste!

> —*JUDY C.*
> *SPRINGFIELD, ILLINOIS*
> 35Y

BATHROOM: GIRLS RULE. You may use it, but it is her bathroom.

> —*SAM*
> *ATLANTA, GEORGIA*
> 3M

TRY AND TEACH YOUR GUYS TO PUT STUFF BACK in the medicine cabinet.

> —*NAN HADDEN*
> *PORTLAND, MAINE*
> 30Y

IN MY NEXT LIFE, I want to come back in a house with my own private bathroom. I don't care how much you love your spouse; you really don't want to be flossing your teeth in their face every night before you go to bed. It is not sexy.

> —*JANICE*
> *CINCINNATI, OHIO*
> 35Y

UH, HELLO? Sitting on the toilet for an hour? How long does it take?

> —*SAMANTHA*
> *ATLANTA, GEORGIA*
> 1Y

A 13-year American study of middle-aged women found that those in good marriages were less likely to develop cardiovascular disease risk factors than unmarried women or those in unsatisfying marriages.

—*HEALTH PSYCHOLOGY*

MOST OF THE HOUSEWORK IS MY JOB because I stay home. I don't have a problem with that. But if I need help, I ask. If I have 5 loads of laundry, I'll bring it upstairs and we'll do it together watching television. You have to ask. You can't expect your husband to instinctively know.

> —*M. BECKERING*
> *SYRACUSE, NEW YORK*
> 💗8Y

• • • • • • • • •

WHEN WE FIRST GOT MARRIED 9 YEARS AGO, my husband and I assumed the traditional husband/wife household chores: I cooked and cleaned and he took care of the yard. Over time, though, our tasks have really evolved, as we discovered the chores that we *preferred*, over the ones we had assumed. For example, my husband is a really good cook—and he really enjoys cooking. So he cooks for our family as much as he can, and because I'd far rather clean up than cook, I take care of the dishes.

> —*JAN*
> *ALLENTOWN, PENNSYLVANIA*
> 💗9Y

• • • • • • • • •

LOOK AT BOTH SIDES OF THE COIN. Some of your wife's traits may drive you crazy, but it may be those same traits that you love. My wife likes to move around and travel which can be tiring, but it also has made my life much more interesting and fun than it would've been with somebody else!

> —*S.M.P.*
> *PORTLAND, MAINE*
> 💗14Y

All in the Family: Dealing with In-Laws

When they're good, they're very, very good, but when they're bad, they're horrid. Yes, we're talking about dear old dad-in-law and his wife, mommy-dearest-in-law. Some couples' families meld together naturally, and others take decades to start talking. But whether you like them or not, they are your family now, and they will be grandparents to your kids, so you'd better learn how to deal with them, even if it means gritting your teeth and losing a little sleep along the way.

WHEN YOUR IN-LAWS VISIT, plan some activities to get out of the house—everyone has a good time and relaxes. And the more relaxed your spouse is, the happier you'll be.

—JASON WAXMAN
SAN JOSE, CALIFORNIA
3Y

WHEN YOU MARRY HIM, YOU MARRY HIS FAMILY.

—WHITNEY KLINCK
PLYMOUTH, MINNESOTA
1Y

How do you
deal with your
in-laws? Ear
plugs.

—*M.B.*
CHARLESTON,
SOUTH CAROLINA
13Y

MY FATHER-IN-LAW, WHO TOTALLY INTIMIDATES ME, has lectured me on what to do with my marriage twice, without being asked. Finally I told him to stay out of our business. He despises me now, but I'm not hearing his opinions on our relationship now, either. And I'm not losing sleep about it either.

—*PHIL*
NEW YORK, NEW YORK
5Y

• • • • • • • •

ANYONE WHO SAYS, "YOU ARE MARRYING the person, not their family" has done you a great disservice. It is crucial to try to get along with them. Put yourself in their place as much as possible. Try to realize where they are coming from when you react to them. I am not like my mother-in-law at all, but we try to capitalize on the things we have in common.

—*JANE ROSENBOHM*
PEORIA, ILLINOIS
35Y

• • • • • • • •

WHEN DEALING WITH YOUR IN-LAWS, I think it's important to think of the love that you feel for your kids. That's how your in-laws feel about your spouse. I didn't understand this until the first time I felt my daughter was in real danger. I felt that she-tiger rush of adrenaline, like I would take a bullet for her. It's humbling to think that your parents feel that way for you, and that's how your spouse's parents feel, too. Even if they are being unreasonable, they may just be acting out of love or a sense of protectiveness. You have to understand and respect that.

—*MARIA ISBELL*
AUSTIN, TEXAS
13Y, 6Y, 3Y

DON'T INTERFERE WITH THEIR FAMILY MATTERS. It is best to be neutral and just support your spouse.

> —PATRICIA
> BROOKLYN, NEW YORK
> 16Y

• • • • • • • •

RESIST THE TEMPTATION TO NITPICK about your honey with your mother-in-law, unless she starts. And never, EVER take it further than she does. You can disagree with your mother-in-law about religion, politics, sports, the weather—anything. But she basically feels she gave up custody of her child to you, and you don't want the tiniest doubt in her mind that you are extremely happy about it.

> —A.S.
> BOSTON, MASSACHUSETTS
> LESS THAN 1Y

• • • • • • • •

AFTER WE GOT MARRIED, my husband and I made it a point to have dinner with my parents once every week or two. That way, we were able to let them know what was going on in our lives without them hounding us for information about what was new.

> —JEAN ROBERTSON
> GLENVIEW, ILLINOIS
> 4Y

• • • • • • • •

I ASKED A FANTASTIC ELDERLY WOMAN I knew how she managed the in-law thing in her day, and her reply became my mantra in dealing with the people I call "the outlaws": "You need to be civil, but strange." For your spouse's sake you MUST remain civil and maintain the relationship, but to remain somewhat sane you need to keep your distance.

> —ANONYMOUS
> PORTLAND, MAINE
> 15Y

As I WRITE THIS, MY FATHER-IN-LAW has just been diagnosed with leukemia. It is a very hard time for our family. But because we have strived for closeness and meaning in our relationship with them, the love just blossoms more. Life is short—treasure them and they will treasure you.

—A.H.
HIGHLAND, NEW YORK
24Y

. . . .

" Have you ever heard of a Sonny-Do List? My father-in-law never had a son of his own. Now he can finally supervise the relocation of his big-screen TV to his upstairs bedroom. "

—B.P.
ORLANDO, FLORIDA
3Y

. . . .

No MATTER WHAT YOU THINK OF YOUR IN-LAWS, they are still your spouse's parents. In the best of all worlds, they will embrace you, and make you feel loved and welcome. In the real world, that doesn't always occur, so make the best of it and remember that no matter how loyal your spouse is, at times, they will be very torn between your needs and the needs of their parents.

—JANICE
CINCINNATI, OHIO
35Y

I'VE FOUND IT HELPS TO LET YOUR SPOUSE take the lead in difficult situations with your in-laws. I have two sets of in-laws because my husband's parents are divorced and both remarried. The two couples are completely different. My husband has a very good relationship with his mother and step-dad, but he doesn't get along so well with his dad and step-mom. And, of course, his mom and step-dad and dad and step-mom don't get along with each other. We do the best we can, but it's always stressful on those occasions when we're all together. What I try to do is take a step back and let my husband handle situations with his parents as he wants, then I follow his lead.

—*ANONYMOUS*
MACUNGIE, PENNSYLVANIA
💔*5Y*

. . . .

FROM THE GET-GO, I BECAME MY MOTHER-IN-LAW'S Enemy Number One. She didn't like me and she didn't have a tough time letting me know. She wouldn't get into a conversation with me; she wouldn't even look at me sometimes. And I wouldn't let it go. Immaturely, I would play her game. I should have walked away, but I wouldn't back down. I would tell her when she was in the wrong and she would be shocked. It was like that for years, until one day she called me and when I picked up the phone I heard that she was crying. She said she wanted to talk to me. She said she was sorry for being so mean and she would really like for me to forgive her. I said, "It has been a number of years. But I accept your apology. It's brave for you to do this." I wasn't prepared for that, but it's been nicer ever since.

—*ARMAND*
SAN DIEGO, CALIFORNIA
💔*5Y*

WHEN YOU CONSIDER MARRYING SOMEBODY, make sure you pay attention to who your in-laws are and whether you can get along with them, because you're going to be spending a lot of time with them.

—*LISA*
CHARLOTTE, NORTH CAROLINA
3Y

• • • • • • • • •

WHEN I LOOK AT MY IN-LAWS I have to make a conscious decision to either focus on the positive things about them or to stew about the negatives. They are just like anybody else that you come in contact with. They have good characteristics and they have flaws. Just like you. If you want to dwell on the negative it will just lead to bad things. Why not try and concentrate on the good traits that they have passed on to your spouse?

—*B.*
ZELIENOPLE, PENNSYLVANIA
2Y

• • • • • • • • •

GET INTO THE ACT

One of the first times I met my husband's parents was at his college graduation. His dad is a professional photographer and his whole family is camera shy. His dad was shooting with the video camera and everyone was ducking behind trees or each other. I walked right up and asked, "Can I give the introductions?" It was love at first sight. His family was so happy to have someone to take away the spotlight they never wanted and his father was happy to finally have a willing and eager on-air talent.

—*AMANDA*
ATLANTA, GEORGIA
2Y

I'VE FOUND GETTING ALONG WITH MY IN-LAWS to be easier and more pleasant since I've had children. It helps me feel more patient with them when I think about the intense love I feel for my children and realize that my in-laws surely have had similar feelings for their son, my husband, even though they don't show it in a way that resonates with me. They come from cultures in which a parent's duties are to make sure their child's physical needs are met and that they can succeed in life. Period. There's no emphasis on a child's emotional health or happiness at all, which is not how I was raised. But I've now come to accept that my in-laws' single biggest way of showing love is to prepare huge quantities of authentic Chinese food. And we make them happiest when we absolutely stuff ourselves, telling them all the while how much we love their food. It took me a few years to catch on to this.

—*D.*
RIVERSIDE, ILLINOIS
14Y

. . . .

I USED TO NOT GET ALONG WITH MY IN-LAWS but finally I wrote them a letter and told them about how I felt about the way they treated me compared to my sister-in-law. I don't know if it worked, but they eventually accepted me anyway. I guess they realized I wasn't going anywhere and I wasn't going to change either.

—*ANONYMOUS*
HASLET, TEXAS
7Y

. . . .

JUST BE YOURSELF WITH YOUR IN-LAWS and don't try too hard.

—*TONYA LEE*
MOUNT AIRY, MARYLAND
11Y

To maintain good relations with your in-laws, move far, far away.

—*ANONYMOUS*
JEFFERSON CITY, MISSOURI
7Y

LET THE IN-LAWS KNOW WHAT'S GOING ON in your life. The more they ask about you or your spouse or the kids, the more annoyed you'll be. Send them cards and pictures so they know what's new. That way, you and your spouse won't have to fight about who's going to update them (especially if they live out of town.)

—PAT AHERN
CHICAGO, ILLINOIS
💔12Y

• • • • • • • •

SURE, MY WIFE AND I BOTH SPEAK ENGLISH, but our words don't have quite the same meaning. She says, "We have to talk." Translation: "You have to listen to me." She says, "You don't spend any time with me." Translation: "We need to do more of the things I like." She says, "My family's coming at the end of the month." Translation—oh, wait. There are many translations for this one, and they depend a little on context. For instance, if winter's coming and I'm getting a little shaggy around the ears, the translation is, "Get a haircut." Or, since I've been restoring our 220-year old farmhouse for a while, the translation is, "Finish everything in the house NOW! And while you're at it, get a haircut!" Finally, since I've been known to be a little cool toward her family, the translation is, "Be polite, or we'll have to talk afterward. And, before I forget, HAIRCUT!"

—RICHARD G. CALO
EAGLE BRIDGE, NEW YORK
💔8Y

• • • • • • • •

HAVE AN OPEN MIND WITH YOUR IN-LAWS. You will learn a lot from how they do things to incorporate into your marriage.

—CASSIE DEMILLE
FAIRCHILD AIR FORCE BASE, WASHINGTON
💔4Y

MY WIFE AND I TAKE A VACATION WITH our in-laws once a year, if we can. It's great because when you're traveling, everything is more relaxed, fun and out in the open.

—*T. OLSEN*
ELMHURST, ILLINOIS
6Y

. . . .

" Marry an orphan. Then you don't have to deal with any in-laws. Wouldn't that be nice? "

—*C.*
PITTSBURGH, PENNSYLVANIA
20Y

. . . .

WHEN MY WIFE AND I FIRST GOT MARRIED, I drove two hours each way to work and I was tired and hungry when I got home. I always looked forward to my wife's meals—especially her spaghetti and meatballs. On one occasion, while my in-laws were visiting us, my mother-in-law made her famous chicken soup on the same day my wife had prepared my favorite dinner. My mother-in-law really wanted me to have some soup, but I didn't want to spoil my appetite for spaghetti and meatballs, so I told her I didn't want the soup. Wrong move! She got angry and said, "If you don't eat the soup, I'm going back to Florida." I replied, "If I eat half, will you go to North Carolina?" She laughed and it broke the ice, but it also taught me a valuable lesson: If a woman cooks for you, eat!

—*BERT KEMPE*
JACKSON, NEW JERSEY
32Y

HAPPY HOLIDAYS?

CHRISTMAS WITH THE FAMILY IS DEFINITELY A JUGGLING ACT. We have her dad, who won't travel, and her mom (it takes a crowbar to get her out of her house), who are divorced. We also have my wife's 30-something brother who acts like he's still in his early 20s. Then we have my two daughters from a previous marriage, and they, of course, are trying to see their mother's family and us. I usually get off on Christmas Eve but some of the others don't. It's a serious struggle to find a time that will work for everyone. And it's not unusual for someone to get offended somewhere in the process.

> —*ANONYMOUS*
> *CARLTON, GEORGIA*
> 4Y

• • • • • • • • •

FOR THE HOLIDAYS, ON EVEN YEARS WE GO TO SEE her family for Christmas, and on odd years we visit my family. Whoever doesn't get Christmas with their family gets Easter and Thanksgiving to make family plans.

> —*D.H.*
> *MINNEAPOLIS, MINNESOTA*
> 14Y

BEFORE YOU MARRY HIM/HER, make sure your prospective in-laws like you (best case), will not interfere in your lives (next best case), or that your spouse will take your side if they don't like you at all (worst case). Whether you like it or not, you do not live in a vacuum and unless your spouse can stand up to his/her parents, your marriage will eventually buckle under the strain of constant interference and the resulting fights that ensue.

—*ANONYMOUS*
NEW YORK, NEW YORK
30Y

• • • • • • • •

YOU SHOULD GET TO KNOW YOUR IN-LAWS before you get married. You need to pay very close attention to how your future husband treats his mother, because that's probably the way he'll treat you later in life. The kind of son he is—and the kind of friend he is—will determine very much what kind of husband he is.

—*CATHY RAFF*
MACCABIM, ISRAEL
13Y

• • • • • • • •

MY MOTHER-IN-LAW WAS BIZARRELY COMPETITIVE and always wanted to show me that she was smarter and more cultured than I. At first it was a struggle not to try to prove her wrong, but I eventually warmed to the role of the uncivilized conqueror of her daughter.

—*ANONYMOUS*
ATLANTA, GEORGIA

I HAD A PROBLEM WITH MY HUSBAND'S FAMILY scheduling events when I couldn't be there. I worked nights and weekends and my schedule was hard to work around, but I let everybody know my work schedule months in advance. The last straw was a family birthday party for my husband planned without me. After that, my husband made a point of telling his family he wouldn't go without me.

—COURTNEY ALFORD-POMEROY
ATHENS, GEORGIA
🧡 1Y

. . . .

❝❝Have a child. I had no common ground with my mother-in-law before I became the mother of her grandchild. Now there is so much to talk about, and all the points of contention can be avoided.❞

—M.M.
PORTLAND, MAINE
🧡 14Y

. . . .

WHEN THINGS BREAK IN THE HOUSE or something falls apart in the yard, don't say, "Let me call my father. He'll know what to do." Trust me—it doesn't make your husband feel very good.

—SUE W.
SEATTLE, WASHINGTON
🧡 33Y

REMEMBER THAT YOUR SPOUSE HAS HAD TO DEAL with his/her family for a lot longer than you have. If you don't automatically feel like you fit in or understand the dynamics of your spouse's family, give it some time. You can't make your in-laws act like your own family. If you expect that to happen you'll set yourself up for failure. Accept your in-laws for who they are and go from there.

—AMANDA
GRAND RAPIDS, MICHIGAN
♥ 1Y

• • • • • • • •

MY MOTHER-IN-LAW IS A TRAIN WRECK of an individual: needy, manipulative, you name it. But she really wants her daughter to be happy. On the first Mother's Day after we got married she told me she already had the best Mother's Day gift she could wish for—her daughter had found happiness with me.

—ANONYMOUS
CARLTON, GEORGIA
♥ 4Y

• • • • • • • •

IF THINGS DON'T GO WELL AT FIRST, WORK AT IT. Remember that they love your spouse just as much as you do, but in a different way—parents want the absolute best for their kids, so expect to be held to a very high standard. And no matter what, treat them at least as well as you would your own parents—you have to see them as equivalents to your own, because that's what you'd expect from your wife or husband.

—DAN DUPONT
ARLINGTON, VIRGINIA
♥ 7Y

DO NOT, UNLESS YOU WANT TO END the marriage pretty quickly, give in to the temptation to compare your spouse to their parents' less desirable traits. Make every effort to stifle it before you let it out of your mouth. You can save the day or ruin it.

—*JANICE*
CINCINNATI, OHIO
35Y

• • • • • • • •

THE NICEST THING MY SPOUSE HAS EVER DONE for me is spending time with my grandfather at family functions. My grandpa is in a wheelchair and can't get around without someone pushing it around for him. A lot of times he ends up sitting at a table by himself while people are getting up to get his food. My husband always sits with him and talks so he's not by himself. That's a pretty nice thing.

—*AMANDA*
ATLANTA, GEORGIA
1Y

• • • • • • • •

I suggest patience with the in-laws. They will let their guard down after they get to know you better.

—*JON & ANNEMARIE*
ELMQUIST
WEST PALM
BEACH, FLORIDA
7M

MY HUSBAND'S FAMILY IS SO DIFFERENT from mine. Mine celebrates every birthday, every holiday, every special occasion. My husband is one of five boys and he is lucky if he gets his birthday card in the mail in time for his birthday. So, it's a different mentality and sometimes all my family functions can be a bit much for him. Plus, my family lives nearby and his is in Indiana. So now, he just doesn't go to every single family function here—that's the way we compromise on the issue.

—*CHRISTINE NEWLIN*
NORCUSS, GEORGIA
11Y

I'VE REFRAINED FROM TALKING ABOUT my in-laws—specifically criticizing or finding fault with them. My theory is: Let 'em be—if they have issues with me, or with us as a couple, it's *their* issues, not mine.

—*T.R.*
SAN FRANCISCO, CALIFORNIA
9Y

SPEAK THEIR LANGUAGE— LITERALLY!

MY FIRST LANGUAGE IS ENGLISH, but my husband's primary language is Spanish. Since we both speak English, I didn't think that language would ever be an issue between us. Then I met his family, and they don't speak any English. I wanted to have a good relationship with my in-laws so I decided to learn Spanish. I took classes on my own, then I practiced speaking Spanish with them. They were so pleased that I wanted to learn their language. They made sure to speak more slowly with me so I could more easily understand, but they were never condescending. My husband was thrilled, too. It had the unexpected benefit of encouraging him to do more for me!

—*N.E.*
HOUSTON, TEXAS
19Y

. . . .

BE CAREFUL WHAT YOU SAY TO YOUR IN-LAWS. My mother-in-law doesn't speak English and is a little hard of hearing. The other day she was telling me in Spanish that her son was going to camp, which was good because he is a bit *gordo* (fat). To make him feel less uncomfortable, I said, "Me, too." My mother-in-law frowned. She thought I had said, "*Y tu*" (So are you).

—*ZAK CERNOCH*
SAN ANTONIO, TEXAS

MY IN-LAWS ARE TURNING INTO OUT-LAWS. I really can't stand to be around them. When I have to see them I just try to avoid them as much as possible. I find a quiet little corner of the house and just read a book. It does no one any good for us to be fighting in front of everyone else.

—*ROB*
EAST LIVERPOOL, OHIO
11Y

" My mother-in-law wore black to our wedding (an informal summer afternoon garden wedding). That was kind of a sign. "

—*M.C.L.*
CHAPEL HILL, NORTH CAROLINA

THE ONE THING THAT WE DIDN'T DISCUSS before getting married was where we wanted to live and how we would interact with family in the future. Now that we live in London, we have to decide how much time we'll spend flying back to the States and how many times we'll do it and whether we'll spend holidays here or with family. You need to know how important those things are to one another. They are much more important to me than to my husband.

—*K.A.C.*
LONDON, ENGLAND
1Y

TO IN-LAWS: DON'T INTERFERE!

There's one event that has strained our relationship forever. We had our first child, a boy, last year. About a month before he was born, we were considering not getting him circumcised. We're not particularly religious, and medical advice leans towards it not being necessary. Since no anesthetic can be used, I really didn't want to do it. My spouse mentioned this to his parents and they freaked out in the worst sort of way. They're Jewish, and Jews are always circumcised. They told him if we didn't circumcise him we would be betraying 6,000 years of Jewish heritage, and that they would not consider our son to be their grandson. My husband's dad claimed that circumcision was the key link between all the generations in his family, and he accused me of breaking apart their family. My poor husband was caught in the middle. To make matters worse, in my opinion, his parents are not even religious— they are culturally Jewish and go to High Holidays at a synagogue, but they don't even believe in God!

Soon the entire extended family was dragged into the argument. I felt like I had no choice. We had to do it, or I risked ostracizing my husband and our son from his family. This was the only week during my pregnancy that my blood pressure spiked. I hated and resented them for taking away the first important decision I was to make for my son. It's none of their business, but they made it theirs. We both lost a lot of respect for them. Not only did they force themselves into a decision that wasn't theirs to make, but they did it in a melodramatic and overbearing way, never once discussing it reasonably with us. The real tragedy is that they have lost their son's respect. My husband is completely disappointed and disgusted by their behavior, and they're too self-righteous even to tell. I used to love his parents. It's very sad.

—*Anonymous*
Austin, Texas
3Y

Oh, family events suck — even with the family members we adore. Talk about stress! We are too young for this, but we have taken to bringing wine to any and all family events. We're all much nicer when we're tipsy.

—COURTNEY ALFORD-
POMEROY
ATHENS, GEORGIA
💔1Y

FIND COMMON GROUND WHERE YOU CAN. For example, my mother likes to send out tacky birthday cards. So, my husband sent her one in return and she has adored him ever since. They also have an ongoing card war . . . who can find the "worst" one each year.

—STACI PRIEST
PFLUGERVILLE, TEXAS
💔6Y

. . . .

MAKE SURE YOUR SPOUSE UNDERSTANDS that you are married to *each other* and not necessarily each other's family. Your spouse should be your spouse first, and a daughter or son second.

—ANONYMOUS
ANN ARBOR, MICHIGAN
💔10Y

Married With Children: Fun for the Whole Family

They say nothing that's worthwhile is easy, and that holds true for kids. When you bring them into your marriage, they challenge you, steal your sleep, and then they (if you're lucky) leave you for college a short 18 years later. But they also fill your lives with endless memories, and they bring out sides of your personality —and your spouse's—you hardly knew existed. If you're married with children, read on. It takes a village, and it's almost always a lot of fun.

WHEN TO HAVE KIDS: The 5-year plan worked for us. We decided to enjoy each other before we had kids. I recommend that (though it doesn't have to be 5 years) to all couples getting married!

—DONNA
ALLENTOWN, PENNSYLVANIA
💗13Y

ONE THING THAT KIDS HAVE ADDED TO OUR MARRIAGE: DROOLING.

–B.P.
ORLANDO, FLORIDA
💗3Y

Kids are harder than marriage. Especially teenagers!

—*Hope Cornish*
Denver,
Colorado

BEING MARRIED IS EASY COMPARED TO BEING married with kids. We were married 17 years before our son was born and all of a sudden we saw sides of each other we hadn't seen before. Things his mother used to say started coming out of my husband's mouth, and things my mom used to say started coming out of mine! No matter how well you know each other, you are still going to face challenges like that, but all I can say is: Make sure you are as grounded as possible together as a couple before you even think of adding children to the equation. It changes everything, and fixes nothing.

—*M.C.*
Denver, Colorado
💕 *25Y*

• • • • • • • •

AS SOON AS YOU HAVE A BABY, start having date nights. We still go out twice a week. Get your mother, your in-laws, or best friend to take your kids while you and your spouse go out. My mother lives nearby, so she often takes our kids. Date night is NOT going to Chuck E. Cheese's.

—*Jill*
Fort Collins, Colorado
💕 *9Y*

• • • • • • • •

BEFORE HAVING KIDS, married couples should do as many fun things as possible. Having children is a huge responsibility. Your life will change drastically. My husband and I took a leisurely trip to Italy a couple months before we conceived our first child. We had a wonderful time and created lasting memories. It was also the last extended vacation we've had together—in six years!

—*Jill*
Atlanta, Georgia
💕 *8Y*

OUR KIDS HAVE A BEAUTIFUL ATMOSPHERE at home. They are growing up in a loving, kind home. And my kids are beautiful inside and out. We tell them all the time how special they are. Some kids like to be out with their friends all the time, but we have to push our kids out—they love to be home.

—*ALEEZA CALLNER*
LOS ANGELES, CALIFORNIA
10Y, ; 22Y

• • • • • • • •

WAIT A YEAR OR TWO BEFORE BRINGING KIDS into the picture, if you can. Everybody says the first year of marriage is the hardest. I definitely agree, especially if you haven't previously lived together. I thought I knew everything about my husband. Boy, was I in for a surprise. I thought he was so neat and tidy because his apartment always appeared clean. Well, he was just really good at throwing things in the closet or under the bed before I got there! When I got pregnant early on in our marriage, my hormones were crazy and being a first-time parent is stressful to begin with. Not only were we learning how to be husband and wife and live together, but we had to learn how to be parents, too.

—*E.*
WHITEMAN AIR FORCE BASE, MISSOURI
2Y

• • • • • • • •

WAIT UNTIL LATER IN LIFE TO HAVE CHILDREN. You will appreciate them so much more. When you and your spouse are younger, sometimes your child gets neglected because you are so focused on your careers. I had a child at 38 and I was so much better at parenting at that stage than I was with my younger kids.

—*PAT FONTENOT*
SAN ANTONIO, TEXAS
13Y

14% of 277 men age 40 to 59 said they always size up a woman's potential as a mother on the first date.

—*MATCH.COM*

I THINK ONE OF THE SECRETS OF A SUCCESSFUL marriage is to have children, to love them and care for them and want to build a nest for them, and keep it there forever. Children never get old to their parents, they will always stay children, and it makes the marriage grow stronger.

　　　　—*M.R.*
　　　　ATLANTA, GEORGIA
　　　　🖤 *36Y*

" When you have kids, enjoy watching your spouse grow into a whole new role as a parent. I have loved seeing my husband become a father—I find it so sexy! "

　　—*R.A.*
　　AUSTIN, TEXAS
　　🖤 *3Y*

THERE'S NOTHING WRONG WITH PLANNING time just for you and your spouse. My husband is in the restaurant business, so his schedule is unpredictable. We used to plan a date whenever we could, even if it was just at home. I would light candles and we would have dinner on the floor together in front of the fireplace.

　　　　—*LYNN JONES*
　　　　KIRKLAND, WASHINGTON
　　　　🖤 *13Y*

WE HAD A STANDING WEDNESDAY NIGHT DATE when our kids were little. The ground rule was "No talking about the kids," which, of course, we broke. But we did carve out some time for us as husband and wife, rather than just "Mom & Dad," and kept the communications going.

—*ELAINE FANTLE SHIMBERG*
TAMPA, FLORIDA
💔*42Y*

• • • • • • • •

AS ALL PARENTS KNOW, the first three months of a baby's life are difficult: One day, when our daughter was about 2 months old, my wife started sobbing. She said that the pain of nursing was intolerable. She was clearly exhausted! My wife is not someone who does well on low sleep. We immediately devised a rather complex sleeping/nursing plan. The goal was to find a way for each of us to get at least 5 hours of sleep in a 24-hour period. Seasoned parents know how sweet that sounds. It took one week to implement the plan. It worked, and we felt great because we had tackled the challenge together and truly nurtured each other's sleep. The lesson: Tackling a problem together is immensely rewarding.

—*ANONYMOUS*
MADISON, WISCONSIN
💔*12Y*

• • • • • • • •

FAMILY RITUALS ARE GOOD. They give a sense of permanence and stability to everyone, especially the children. Every Friday night, I bring home Chinese food for dinner. It's a simple gesture, but one that provides a sense of tradition and family closeness. Everyone looks forward to their Moo Goo Gai Pan on Fridays.

—*L.B.*
CINCINNATI, OHIO
💔*35Y*

Make family trips a priority. They build memories.

*—RENAE
ATLANTA, GEORGIA
3Y*

IT'S GREAT TO KEEP DOING FUN THINGS as a couple. My husband grew up in a very conservative family, and they didn't exchange a lot of gifts. So to make more of the gift-giving experience, we have had a lot of treasure hunts. But the best ritual of all is our Halloween costume contest. Each year, my husband and one daughter team up against me and our other daughter. We secretly design costumes for the girls, which are revealed on Halloween. My husband goes all out for this. One year he designed a costume for our older daughter of a bottle of liquid soap—she wore the nozzle on the top of her head! These rituals make our life fun!

*—MOLLY BROWN
ALLENTOWN, PENNSYLVANIA
23Y*

. . . .

SINCE WE HAD KIDS, my husband is the one who takes them to all the crazy things in town like the restaurants with playgrounds inside and the movie theater. I can't stand taking the kids to the movies, so he just does it without me. It's made it much easier because then I can spend time with the kids doing more laid-back activities I feel comfortable with.

*—CATHY
CORALVILLE, IOWA
9Y*

. . . .

WE HAD THE HAPPIEST MOMENT a few nights ago. We were all lying in bed. My husband had one hand on our daughter Siena and one hand on my face. He leaned over and hugged both of us, and I'd never felt more like a real family.

*—ISABELLA BAUHAUS
SANTA CRUZ, CALIFORNIA
3Y*

Do things together. I have so many memories from my childhood of my whole family being together, doing things together. My dad used to jump out of bed on the weekends and say to us, "Get up! You're wasting the day away!" On the spur of the moment, he'd load my mother, brother, sister, and me in the car just to go someplace. We'd drive two hours to Philadelphia for cheese steaks, just to have something to do! Now with my own family, it's unthinkable for my husband and I not to do things together whenever we can, with our children. We even go to the grocery store together—my husband, me, my mother (who lives with us right now), and our three kids. We need to get two carts, but we enjoy doing even these simplest things together as a family.

—*Angela*
Bethlehem, Pennsylvania
9y

. . . .

Avoid car trips! My husband loves to drive so we took a two-week driving vacation. He said that it would be fun to drive leisurely, stopping whenever we wanted, and just enjoying the scenery. Also, he said it would be a different experience than driving to work every day. I imagined us in the car, listening to good music, having impromptu picnics, and talking for hours. It was a nightmare! My husband insisted on "making good time" to get to our next destination though we weren't on any schedule. He stopped only for gas—no food, picnics, no historic sites. One day, we drove for 12 hours straight. Then he wanted to start driving at night, too, taking turns at the wheel.

—*M.K.*
Houston, Texas
21y

KIDS AND SECOND MARRIAGES

MY KIDS WERE SO ANXIOUS for us to get married that I think it was a relief when we finally decided to actually do it. My daughter was excited to be a flower girl. That was her first question and concern. She was focused on herself, as 12-year-old girls are. My younger son was quite excited, but he also needed reassuring that he was still going to have his same "place" with me. My eldest son was relieved, elated, and extremely encouraging. All three of them have wonderful relationships with my new husband. Meantime, his daughter was happy, but it was harder for her. We tried to help her, and all the kids, by keeping day-to-day life "business as usual."

> —*ALLISON LEVYN*
> *BEVERLY HILLS, CALIFORNIA*
> *1Y*

• • • • • • • •

WHEN I MET THE WOMAN who would be my second wife, for the first time in my life I felt a physical, emotional and intellectual bond with a woman. I found a woman who was strong and smart and wanted a partner in life. It sounds strange, but I knew I was in love by the third date and we were engaged after only 5 months. And this comes 2 years after the end of a very bad marriage. I suppose I really matured as a result of my first marriage. I learned to be less selfish, more giving, less demanding. I learned to listen. I learned I couldn't (and shouldn't) have my way all the time.

> —*ANONYMOUS*
> *CARLTON, GEORGIA*
> *24Y*

IF YOU KEEP FEEDING THEM IN THE CAR, giving them things to do, and even sit in the back seat with them, while the other is driving, a lot of kids can go for several hours on car trips. At a place like the beach, everyone can enjoy themselves. I think you have to find activities for the kids and grown-ups to do together, and just make sure you're stopping along the way to let the kids enjoy something. Also, if you tell them ahead of time that you are going to a certain place, and this is how long you'll be there, they are more likely to handle it. On the other hand, sometimes if you give them too much notice, you have to listen to whining.

—*ANONYMOUS*
LOS ANGELES, CALIFORNIA
11Y

• • • • • • • •

OUR FAMILY HAS MANY HAPPY MEMORIES of vacations—particularly trips to Cape Cod during the summer—but several unhappy memories of car trips. One that comes to mind is when my middle daughter threw the oldest daughter's Barbie Doll out the window, and the retaliation was a wad of gum put in the initiator's hair.

—*ANONYMOUS*
WELLESLEY, MASSACHUSETTS
40Y

• • • • • • • •

WE HAVE A 23-YEAR-OLD, a 21-year-old and a 14-year-old. Because we were raised quite differently, we found that trying to mesh parenting styles caused more arguments than money, religion and sex put together. It is very hard to ignore that little voice in your head that keeps saying, "But my dad wouldn't have ever said that!"

—*V.B.*
DOHA, QATAR
28Y

We took the boys to New York to see my parents. And they were so good. But I gave them both Benadryl before we got on the plane!

—*ANONYMOUS*
EDEN PRAIRIE,
MINNESOTA
6Y

MAKE SURE YOU SPEND A LOT OF QUALITY time with hubby before having kids. Once they come, the fun is over for some time.

—*L.S.*
SHARON, MASSACHUSETTS
8Y

• • • • • • • •

" When you and your wife have a new baby, don't bring up your lack of sleep. Even if you're still working and have early meetings and have to be sharp at work—leave that topic alone. The guy is never going to win that argument. "

—*ANONYMOUS*
GREENWICH, CONNECTICUT
2Y

• • • • • • • •

GIVE YOUR HUSBAND SOME OF HIS OWN TIME with the kids. My husband is in charge of bedtime. They like to have bath time with him. He reads to them and, most of the time, he puts them to bed. Also, Saturday is his day with the boys. They go to the gym and shop and go out to lunch. It's a nice routine, and they gain a lot from being with Dad and away from me for a while.

—*ANONYMOUS*
EDEN PRAIRIE, MINNESOTA
6Y

SUPPORTING EACH OTHER IS HUGE. My son said something rude to me this morning at breakfast and my husband just kept on pouring his coffee, not paying any attention. I took him aside and said, "You know, a little help from you would be great. Can't you back me up when I'm trying to teach our son right from wrong?" My husband agreed with me, luckily, and promised to pay more attention. I don't know what I would have done if he didn't see that sort of thing the same way as I do.

—M.
DENVER, COLORADO

• • • • • • • •

THE BIGGEST MISTAKE I MADE is not backing my wife up when she was dealing with the kids. Too many times I've taken the side of the kids and not heard her out. I should have said, "Listen to Mom and we'll talk about it later." It can be a sticking point in the marriage. Don't disagree with your spouse in front of your kids. Sticking up for each other shows the kids Mom and Dad respect each other. It's also teaching the kids to respect both of you.

—J.G.
SYRACUSE, NEW YORK
💕21Y

• • • • • • • •

OUR TWO CHILDREN, AGES 10 AND 12, are almost as opposite in their ways as we are in ours. And they get along beautifully. It's more fun to appreciate quirks than quibble over differences.

—GRACIELA SHOLANDER
FORT COLLINS, COLORADO
💕15Y

MY HUSBAND AND I HAVE TWO GIRLS who are only 15 months apart. Our daughters are both great, but their personalities are as different as night and day. My husband had a hard time understanding that the girls are so different that they need to be parented differently. He takes more of a "drill sergeant" approach with both girls. This works fine for one, but not the other. This caused quite a bit of stress in our marriage as I struggled to help him to understand that he needed to discipline them differently. I was patient and explained this to him. Over time I think that by watching me he's gotten much better!

—*DONNA*
ALLENTOWN, PENNSYLVANIA
13Y

• • • • • • • •

" Back each other up when disciplining your children. United we stand, divided we fall. "

—*ANONYMOUS*
TAMPA, FLORIDA
24Y

• • • • • • • •

WHEN I GOT MARRIED A SECOND TIME, my husband had two kids from a previous marriage and I had three. Mutual respect and communication are very important factors when combining families. Communication is important between two families and as parents you have to apply the same set of rules to everyone.

—*J.L.*
CHICAGO, ILLINOIS
, , 20Y

WATCH WHAT YOU SAY

I was in the first year of my surgery residency in Chicago. My wife and I had taken up residence in a Chicago suburb along with our two children. Our daughter, the older of the two, was around 4 years old. First-year residents are "low man on the Totem Pole," so I had duty at the hospital all day and every other night. It was a tiring routine, but we had youth on our side, and hope for better prospects.

One night I brought home a nurse friend from the hospital to baby-sit the children while my wife and I went out for an evening together. This was the first time my children had met a nurse. My daughter was fascinated, and she soon found out all the details about how the nurse worked at the hospital where I worked, and how we knew each other, and how nurses also took care of sick people at the hospital.

Several days later a salesman came to our apartment, and my daughter answered the door. The salesman asked if he could see her daddy or mommy. My wife, who was working in the kitchenette just around the corner, heard my daughter answer, "My daddy is not here. He is at the hospital sleeping with the nurses." My wife dropped what she was doing and came to the door quickly. We had a good laugh about it later.

—Dr. & Mrs. R.B. Scheidt
Van Wert, Ohio
43Y

FAMILY OUTINGS

EACH MONTH WE PLAN A "FAMILY DAY," where we set aside a day to do something special together like going on a picnic, to the movies, or on a day trip. Our plan is also to take a vacation every year, taking turns picking where we go. On even-numbered years, she picks, so it will probably be Disney. And on odd-numbered years, I pick, so we'll go to NASCAR.

> —*MICHAEL REICH*
> *HELLERTOWN, PENNSYLVANIA*
> 1Y

• • • • • • • • •

WHEN THE OPPORTUNITY COMES UP TO GO ON VACATION, the Mom part of me wants to bring our kids along. My husband refuses, constantly reminding me that the kids will grow up and eventually move away, but the two of us will be together forever, so we need special time alone together. Leaving the kids at home was difficult to get used to at first, but now, almost every vacation is like another honeymoon. It's important to start doing this when the kids are young, so they immediately get the message.

> —*S.H.*
> *NEW LENOX, ILLINOIS*
> 20Y

• • • • • • • • •

HERE'S AN EASY WAY TO HAVE FUN AS A COUPLE and bring the kids along—go to the drive-in! When our kids were small, instead of trying to take them to the movies or having to hire a babysitter, we simply took them along to the drive-in movies. That way, the kids could play or sleep in the backseat. It didn't matter if they were noisy. When they were really small, I could even comfortably nurse them in the privacy of our car.

> —*MOLLY BROWN*
> *ALLENTOWN, PENNSYLVANIA*
> 23Y

OUR BEST FAMILY VACATION WAS WHEN WE WENT to Niagara Falls with one child. The trip included my little sister. We camped, we fine-dined, we had a built-in babysitter, we saw beautiful sites, and the weather was awesome.

—*NINA*
MARIETTA, GEORGIA
7Y

• • • • • • • •

PLAN FAMILY VACATIONS AS A COUPLE. Work together to make sure that each of you gets to do the things that you really want to do. Make sure to schedule some down time for your family to just rest and relax. Don't try to do too much in one vacation. I planned our first trip to Disney World mostly by myself. The schedule was way too overloaded. I felt like I was dragging my family from one event to the next until we were exhausted. But the second time we went, we planned the trip together as a couple, and even had input from our children. We made sure to do the important stuff each person wanted to do, and also left time to just relax by the pool.

—*KEVIN SHOLANDER*
FORT COLLINS, COLORADO
15Y

• • • • • • • •

I SAY YOU SHOULD LEAVE THE PLANNING of the family vacations to your husband. That way he has to take all the blame when things go wrong. And don't things always go wrong with those trips?

—*BETTY SMITH*
PITTSBURGH, PENNSYLVANIA
40Y

Before you have kids, buy a dog. It's great training.

—*RICHARD HALL*
KENNESAW,
GEORGIA
💔 *10Y*

MY HUSBAND AND I DECIDED EARLY ON that it's critical to present a united front to our children—especially if you have more than two, like us, and are outnumbered. We agreed to stand by each others' decisions. We've taught our daughters that they are not allowed to ask me something and then if I say "no" go ask their father the same thing, or vice versa.

—*TORI DENNIS*
IRON CITY, TENNESSEE
💔 *10Y*

• • • • • • • • •

REMEMBER, THE FAMILY IS A UNIT. I've moved to remote places in Brazil, South Africa, and other very isolated places. I had two children during those times. My husband and I learned quickly that we had to be able to rely on each other unconditionally—we were completely dependent upon each other for almost everything. And because of that, I always knew that I could count on him (and vice versa) for anything from how to  help our sick child in a town without a doctor to catching a gigantic roach on the wall of our hut in the rain forest!

—*NANCY*
BRUSSELS, BELGIUM
💔 *40Y*

For Better or Worse: Coping with Life's Biggest Challenges

When you said "for better and worse" on your wedding day, you were probably more focused on the "better" part. But as life goes on and the inevitable crises emerge, you realize how much all that work you've invested in your relationship pays off. When someone's sick, when jobs end, when retirement comes, when the kids are all out of the house, it's your spouse who will be there at the end of the day—you hope!—to help you get through it. Here's some food for thought.

IF YOU LIVE TOGETHER LONG ENOUGH, there will be lots of crises because life is not a smoothly paved road. That's when you really need to stick together. It's easy to be with someone during the fun times. The true test of a marriage is sticking it out during the tough times.

—JANICE
CINCINNATI, OHIO
35Y

INFIDELITY WAS THE HARDEST THING WE FACED. HE FORGAVE. I NEVER FORGAVE MYSELF!

—N.
MARIETTA, GEORGIA
7Y

REMEMBER THE HIGHER PURPOSE. When marriage gets tough, sometimes it's helpful to clarify the most important benefits and purposes of your relationship. Then ask yourself, "If I achieve that purpose, what will I gain?" Once you have identified your higher purpose, you'll gain some perspective really fast.

—*JEAN NICK*
KINTNERSVILLE, PENNSYLVANIA
13Y

• • • • • • • • •

CRISIS CAN TEST A MARRIAGE BUT PANICKING, freaking out, and otherwise losing it doesn't help at all. My husband lost two jobs within a few  years, and due to the recession, it took months to find new work. At the same time, I was also at the end of my pregnancy, so it was a very stressful time. I made sure that we both had space—both physical space, and time. I bit my tongue many times when I wanted to nag him or even help him with the search. And we made sure we spent some positive time together—seeing matinees or going out to lunch.

—*A.T.*
ARLINGTON, MASSACHUSETTS
13Y

• • • • • • • • •

A DEFINITE WARNING SIGN that your spouse might be cheating would be if your spouse is spending more time with other people than he or she is with you. If that's the case, then I'd check into where he or she is going, who they're with and why. You don't want to assume the worst at first, but don't be naïve.

—*DEBBIE L.*
CAMILLUS, NEW YORK
2Y

CRISES WE'VE FACED: job loss, euthanizing pets, Grandmother's death, his daughter's fight with Hodgkin's disease, his other daughter's car accidents, my breast cancer and mastectomy. Basically, we depend on each other. We talk about how the incident makes us feel and then we support one another and tell each other what we need.

—*JAN ALDER*
ATLANTA, GEORGIA
7Y

* * * * * * * *

"I'm a type-B person—very laid back. In fact, I'm almost type-C, which stands for comatose. One day, my wife was telling me about a friend of hers whose husband was going through a mid-life crisis. I paused and replied, "I don't have to have a mid-life crisis, do I?" It's a myth that every guy goes through this. For some of us, the whole idea just seems like too much work."

—*JOE HOLLIMAN*
CENTENNIAL, COLORADO
33Y

DEALING WITH CHEMICAL DEPENDENCY

DO NOT THINK THAT YOU CAN REHABILITATE someone who has a history of drug problems. It just ain't gonna happen. I think women often fall for guys with a history of problems because it's like finding a little puppy with a broken leg. You want to take it home and care for it. But it just doesn't work with people. You cannot fix what is wrong with him or give him what he needs. What he needs is professional help, not a shoulder to cry on.

—RACHEL COSSMAN
SOUTH BEND, INDIANA
5Y

QUITTING SMOKING CAN BE A SERIOUS and unexpected threat to marriage. When my husband quit smoking, he became a bear—irritable, non-communicative, and withdrawn. He even complained that my cooking tasted funny. This lasted about six months. When the withdrawal period finally ended, he returned to his usual, cheerful self, and he enjoys my cooking again, but this period was difficult for me and the children.

—M.S.
TORONTO, CANADA
14Y

PART OF SURVIVING AN ADDICTION is deciding—making a conscious decision—to let all the anger go. It takes time. You have to be very clear about what you need. For me, it was knowing what he was doing, where he was going, when he would be home. It also took open communication about how his addiction affected me and the family. Also, you do have to give it time. It took us about a year and a half to go through the process, and it took counseling on my part as well as the work my husband did on his recovery, and joint counseling.

—L.
KIRKLAND, WASHINGTON
14Y

MANY YEARS AGO, I WAS ON A FAST-TRACK career at IBM, which required me to travel a LOT. My wife, who was an elementary school teacher, eventually got sick of me coming home exhausted and cranky, not wanting to be around other people. After all, she had been locked up with ankle-biters all day and she wanted to go out and do things! Eventually we separated, and when we finally took a vacation together to try and reconcile, she said something that really opened my eyes. She said, "The new guy I've been seeing is everything you're not: fun, carefree, energetic." As painful as her words were, they were what I needed to hear. I realized she was absolutely right. I *had* been too caught up in the corporate chase. Life is all about finding a balance. You have to fig-ure out what's most important to you and make time for it, no matter what.

    —*K.*
    KINGSTON, NEW YORK
    💔10Y

. . . .

WE HAVE ISSUES WITH INFERTILITY and it's been a huge strain on our marriage, an absolute roller coaster of emotions. One day you'll be okay with it and the next day you're a mess. It can make or break you. The stress of lovemaking on demand and timing everything and seeing it not work time and again is very damaging to a marriage. If I could go back I wouldn't have waited 5 years to see a doctor. I would have been more conscious about what was happening and gone to see a doctor in the first year of problems.

    —*M.C.*
    AUSTIN, TEXAS
    💔8Y

MOST DIFFICULT THING IN MARRIAGE: The stress of trying to have a baby. We didn't have problems getting pregnant, but rather staying pregnant. I had an ectopic pregnancy and had to have all these surgeries and my own health was becoming an issue. There was the loss of work and wages as a result. The stress of the situation kind of took the fun out of sex. Getting so uptight about getting pregnant doesn't help the situation at all.

—*J.B.H.*
ALEXANDRIA, VIRGINIA
2Y

• • • • • • • •

YOU HAVE TO BE SUPPORTIVE OF YOUR SPOUSE no matter what. The two of you really are a team. If he really wants to do something—like change jobs—that at first blush you are not sure about, you still have to be supportive. Hopefully he is the same way with you. When I told my husband that I wanted to go back to school a couple years ago I was worried about what he might say. But he was behind me 100 percent and that made me feel wonderful.

—*CHARLENE DEPASQUALE*
PITTSBURGH, PENNSYLVANIA
21Y

• • • • • • • •

I WAS WITH THE SAME WOMAN for 11 years, married to her for 1 year. She was unfaithful with my best friend. I kicked her out. You have to have a lot of faith if you're with somebody for that long. Everybody thinks the person they're with long-term would never, ever do anything like that, but it's not always true.

—*ANONYMOUS*
ATLANTA, GEORGIA
1Y,

THE 7-YEAR ITCH WON'T HAPPEN if you have different interests. My husband and I are 8 years into our marriage and are doing fine because we pursue our own interests, friends and activities while still spending time with each other. I don't have to be with him every weekend and vice versa. I make plans with girlfriends or take mini-vacations with them to get out of town for a night or two. It makes the time we do spend together more special.

—*STACI KESSLER*
HIGHLAND PARK, ILLINOIS
8Y

• • • • • • • •

IF YOU'RE THINKING ABOUT LEAVING your marriage to find someone better, know that there is no "better," just different. Someone told me this and it has been very helpful. I think for us, staying married all this time (and we've had our difficulties) has had a lot to do with taking the commitment seriously. We feel like the commitment we have made is central to who we are and if we couldn't make that work, we would be disappointed.

—*NAOMI NEMTZOW*
BROOKLYN, NEW YORK
24Y

• • • • • • • •

BE ON GUARD WITH YOUR SPOUSE at high school and college school reunions. That is a time for temptations, when many people rekindle relationships with old boyfriends and girlfriends. My husband renewed his relationship with his old college girlfriend at that time. He divorced me and eventually married her.

—*ANONYMOUS*
SAN ANTONIO, TEXAS
25Y, 5Y

Just remember, whatever it is that you're going through, you'll come out stronger on the other side.

—*JWAlll*
ATLANTA, GEORGIA
9Y

TRY TO FIND THE POSITIVE in challenging situations. When my husband lost his job of 19 years, it was quite a blow. But we've tried to look at it as an opportunity—for him to get all those projects done he's always wanted to do around the house. It's keeping him busy as he goes back to school and prepares for his next career. Completing those tasks also gives my husband a sense of accomplishment.

—*M.*
ALLENTOWN, PENNSYLVANIA
💔23Y

• • • • • • • •

" Cheat?!? Are you kidding me? My husband is seriously hot and he thinks the same of me. "

—*K.R.*
WEST WINDSOR, NEW JERSEY
💔11Y

• • • • • • • •

AFTER 7 YEARS OF MARRIAGE, we had become distant with each other. I, in rather typical male fashion, started a serious flirtation with a woman at work. Of course, this accomplished nothing but discomfort and pain all around. Fortunately, it did not progress, but the damage to our marriage was evident. Couples counseling ensued. It was here that we learned about the need to express our feelings directly. This was a hard, painful lesson.

—*ANONYMOUS*
MADISON, WISCONSIN
💔12Y

COPING WITH THE EX

ON MANY LEVELS I LIKE HIS EX. But I don't like having her in our life. Many times plans with his children have been decimated by her inability to stick to a schedule or consider our needs.

> —JAN ALDER
> ATLANTA, GEORGIA
> 💔 7Y

• • • • • • • •

I THINK THE BIGGEST THING WITH DIVORCE—when you have kids and money involved—is to remain friends. You will see your ex again; your children will get married and you will stand up there with him or her. With my ex-husband, we are open with each other and I wish him the best. It was difficult at the beginning, but that passed. We are good friends and we understand each other.

> —ALEEZA CALLNER
> LOS ANGELES, CALIFORNIA
> 💔 10Y, 💔; 💔 22Y

• • • • • • • •

BE FRIENDS WITH THE EX if you want the relationship with the step-child to work. At least that way you know who she is and she knows who you are and she doesn't have to worry that you're going to steal her kid away. I knew I could never be friends with her until my husband and I were married—she had to know it was a done deal and that I was here to stay.

> —CATHY RAFF
> MACCABIM, ISRAEL
> 💔 13Y

Men "marry down." Males, especially those tying the knot for the second time, generally choose younger wives (by at least 5 years) who are lower in professional status. Dr. Freud? Comments?

—*Minneapolis Star Tribune*

ON INFIDELITY: Think Lorraine Bobbitt, not Hillary Clinton. OK, just kidding, but the fact is that trust is a crucial element in any strong marriage. Hurt feelings are easy enough to come by when you live with somebody for any length of time, so a betrayal as big as infidelity can be extremely destructive. Think before you act.

—*L.B.*
CINCINNATI, OHIO
35Y

· · · · · · · ·

MY HUSBAND PASSED AWAY after 37 years of marriage. He was diagnosed with cancer and died 10 months later. Those 10 months were filled with chemotherapy, radiation, and fear. But also lots of love. I made sure to remember the happy times and to laugh with him. We had to remember that the cancer was not everything and did not define our relationship. But we often had to remind the other person of this fact—often he reminded me. Life-threatening or terminal illness is incredibly difficult. But we made the most out of the time we had left together.

—*NANCY NEIBERG KOSANOVICH*
NAGS HEAD, NORTH CAROLINA
37Y

· · · · · · · ·

MY MOTHER-IN-LAW'S HUSBAND DIED. I supported my husband immediately getting on a plane and going to the funeral, so he could be with his mother. I couldn't go because we had a young baby at the time, and it was most important for him to be there. It's hard, but the best thing is to try to draw closer to each other instead of drawing inside of yourself.

—*ANONYMOUS*
LOS ANGELES, CALIFORNIA
11Y

WHEN THERE'S BEEN A DEATH IN THE FAMILY, don't make any jokes whatsoever. They won't go over well. My wife and I were really broke, so when I found out we'd have to fly to Indiana when her grandmother died, I kidded around about taking advantage of the situation to score discount airfare. She responded with dead silence, then later turned extremely upset. Seven years later, this is still a touchy subject.

—*RANDY*
PEORIA, ILLINOIS
8Y

• • • • • • • •

I HAD TO GO GET SOME MEDICAL TESTS DONE and I was very worried and my husband couldn't go with me. He wrote me a note and stuck it in my car and after I read that I felt a whole lot braver. It made me feel like he'd be there with me.

—*JANE*
BROOKLYN, NEW YORK
20Y

• • • • • • • •

TWO OF MY HUSBAND'S TEETH UNEXPECTEDLY turned blue, so he went to the dentist. The news was devastating: Alan was diagnosed with a very rare form of cancer. Within a 9-month period, he had to undergo numerous surgeries, chemotherapy and special out-of-state radiation treatments. Fortunately, with lots of prayer, support and great medical advice, we got through this. He has been in remission for 3 years. Things like filling up your social calendar, having a perfectly clean house and owning the latest material goods don't really matter. What's important is that you're always there for your family.

—*ROBYN MURAMOTO*
CENTENNIAL, COLORADO
19Y

IN SICKNESS AND IN HEALTH

One of the biggest crises any couple faces in a marriage is that of serious illness. I couldn't imagine facing that without the support and love of my husband. I was 49 when I was diagnosed with Stage 1 breast cancer. While I was going through all the phases of this disease—diagnosis, acceptance, surgery, radiation and finally chemotherapy—it was my husband who served as my "rock." He was the one I held onto, many times in the literal sense. Although I was fortunate to have family, friends and colleagues who were part of my support group as well, it was my spouse whose strength I used to help me through every day and every night of emotional and physical distress. If it hadn't been for him, I would have never made the decisions I made. It was my husband who took me to other oncologists for second and third opinions. It was my husband whose hand I held before the surgery. It was my husband who helped me through the radiation for six weeks following the surgery. It was my hus- band who got me up the stairs when my body didn't want to go to every chemotherapy session, trying to tell jokes and divert me from the discom- fort of the treatments. It was my husband who listened with love and understanding when I went through each stage of the disease and its recovery. It was my husband who encour- aged me to volunteer and help support other women as he had helped to support me. It's my husband who walks with me every Mother's Day for the Y-Me Walk/Race against breast cancer and who continues to love and cherish me every day. Every day begins and ends with him. He is truly a gift in my life!

—DEE
OAK LAWN, ILLINOIS
36Y

THE LARGEST CRISIS I FACED WAS FINDING out my first wife had a terminal illness. It changed our entire life plan. You know that you won't be sitting on the porch when you retire, watching the grandkids, etc. As devastating as the news is, however, there is the gift of knowing that because the time you have together may be short, you should cherish all the moments you do have. We can become caught up in all the hectic aspects of life and fail to see the greater meaning of love, giving and caring. So, you shift your priorities. You relish the good days and get through the tough ones; do what you can, when you can, and try to imprint each and every one of those precious moments in your memory because you know they are fleeting.

—*R.A.*
CEDAR RAPIDS, IOWA
♥25Y

• • • • • • • •

THE YEAR AFTER WE MARRIED, her dad had congestive heart failure followed by quadruple bypass surgery. A couple of years ago my mother died. When things like that happen you drop what you're doing and do what you can to help your spouse deal with the crisis. We essentially lived at the hospital for a couple of weeks when her dad's crisis hit. After my mother's death, we faced a 4-day ordeal of arranging the funeral, dealing with my irate brother, guests from out of town, and the list goes on. When a crisis hits your spouse, it's your turn to give. Love, support, help them be firm when needed, give them space if they need it. Support them. And hope you both have understanding employers.

—*ANONYMOUS*
CARLTON, GEORGIA
♥4Y

WE LOST OUR MIDDLE CHILD, our son, when he was 4 months old. He had a rare genetic disorder. It was really hard on our marriage but I don't think either one of us considered giving each other up. We had a hard time talking about it and we still do. I read somewhere that 95 percent of couples who lose children also lose their marriages. We've had the cards stacked against us. But what got me through it was reading books about angels, and believing that he's still out there, up in heaven. As far as our marriage goes, it's stronger than it's ever been. It's scarred; we're both scarred. But we've both been through it together.

—K.J.
ST. AUGUSTINE, FLORIDA
9Y

• • • • • • • •

MY FATHER DIED IN 1997. My wife did everything right. She took a week off of work to travel with me to Oregon. She was with me as I watched my father's life slip away. She helped with funeral arrangements, helped coordinate everything, and rallied her family to support me during the service in Wisconsin. She left me alone when I needed time by myself, and listened when I needed to talk. The lesson: Pull out all the stops. Do whatever your spouse needs. You don't get a second chance to help someone grieve a death in the family.

—ANONYMOUS
MADISON, WISCONSIN
12Y

AFTER WE WERE MARRIED A FEW YEARS, my husband became very ill. He was in the hospital for 3-1/2 months, and our world was turned upside down. At the time, the most important thing to us was for my husband to get better. I'd drive 1-1/2 hours each way 4 times a week to visit him at the hospital, on top of working full time and keeping our household running. When I visited, we forced ourselves to count our blessings. Quite literally, we listed them out loud. Sometimes the best we could do was to be thankful that our old car didn't break down during the drive, and we'd laugh because that was the best we could come up with. In some ways it was the best thing that ever happened to us. Having survived that, we know we can survive anything.

—*JENNY*
DENTON, TEXAS
 12Y

- - - - - - - - -

TO COPE WITH THE DEATH OF MY HUSBAND, I joined a bereavement group. I resisted initially because I thought it would be a group of sad people meeting to have a "crying party." It was absolutely different. Yes, people did cry sometimes. And, yes, we did laugh sometimes. But mostly we admired each other for sharing the grieving process as well as the coping process. I saw very distraught people get better. I got better. I learned how to continue to live and thrive. I highly recommend grief counseling as a group or individual therapy. Most importantly, get the help you need.

—*NANCY NEIBERG KOSANOVICH*
NAGS HEAD, NORTH CAROLINA
37Y

> Most people who lost a spouse but did not remarry took about 8 years to recover emotionally.
>
> —*CNN*

REMEMBER THAT YOU MADE A PROMISE: Just a few years after my husband and I were married, he had a terrible parachuting accident. His right leg was amputated below his knee. Our marriage was almost torn apart. My husband was in so much pain that he pushed me away. How did I get through it? I focused on my promise. I had vowed to love him in sickness and in health, and I reminded myself of that promise constantly. Also, I kept a wedding picture in the place where I spent most of my time—in the kitchen! I looked at it all of the time. It reminded me of why we had gotten married in the first place—because we loved each other more than anything else. It was such a dark time in our lives, but we got through it, and our marriage has thrived over the years.

—*TORI DENNIS*
IRON CITY, TENNESSEE
♥ *10Y*

● ● ● ● ● ● ● ●

OUR BIGGEST CHALLENGE CAME after 10 years of marriage. We had married very young—right out of high school. Then, in our late twenties, we both began to wonder if there was something that we had missed—maybe there was someone better out there. So, we separated for 3 months, during which time we dated other people and lived our own lives. It didn't take long before we practically ran back into each others' arms. We'd had a good time, but discovered that life simply was not as good without the other person in it. Twenty-four years later, we still only have eyes for each other. I knew that it was a big risk to our marriage, but it was a risk we had to take.

—*N.*
WILLIAMSBURG, VIRGINIA
♥ *34Y*

MY HUSBAND HAD HIS FIRST OPEN-HEART surgery when he was 43. The doctors warned me that male patients especially tend to undergo drastic personality changes after open-heart surgery because they're frustrated about not being as strong and healthy as they "should" be. I didn't believe this would happen to my husband, who'd always been so easy-going. However, immediately after the surgery, all of this anger started seeping out of him. It got to the point where he'd blow up any time our boys did the littlest thing wrong. Fortunately, after about a year, his anger dissolved. My advice to anyone whose spouse has undergone open-heart surgery is to take advantage of the educational programs at your hospital. If they had been available during my husband's surgery, maybe the stress and tension wouldn't have lasted for so long.

—JOAN
CENTENNIAL, COLORADO
40Y

Expect problems. Hope for problems! I know it sounds strange to say that, but problems help a person—and a couple—to grow.

—*PAGET PERRAULT*
MELBOURNE,
AUSTRALIA
36Y

WHEN YOUR SPOUSE IS GOING THROUGH a personal crisis, love him or her, but get a life. It is impossible to share everything that you are going through. Even though you are going through it together, there are parts that you will have to experience alone. And you have to be able to get away from the crisis from time to time so that you have some strength to come back to the marriage.

—*ELAINE LANG*
NEW BRAUNFELS, TEXAS
6Y

EMPTY NEST

WHEN YOUR KIDS ARE ALL GROWN UP and out of the house, you actually have to figure out how to love your wife again. The first year is always the hardest, but it gets easier.

—*D.*
CEDAR RAPIDS, IOWA
35Y

• • • • • • • • •

DON'T BE SO SURE YOU'RE GOING TO HAVE AN EMPTY NEST. My two kids have gone and come back a lot. It's hard when they go off on their own. I dreaded their new lives, worrying that I wouldn't be there all of the time to protect them. But then that fear wears off, and when they come back, you feel like your world has been invaded! Also, when kids move away, they don't take their stuff with them! Our basement is a furniture warehouse. I don't know if we're ever going to have an empty nest because it's still so full of stuff!

—*ANONYMOUS*
LONG VALLEY, NEW JERSEY
35Y

• • • • • • • • •

EMPTY NEST: My first thought was "HOORAY! Now let's do whatever we want, whenever we want." But it doesn't always work that way. It actually is a very sad time, and one that a mother especially feels, because she no longer feels "needed," and her hands-on mothering is done. In time, you do learn, however, that what you really want is for your child to grow into a mature, responsible adult—so, get over it!

—*NOLA SMITH*
TAMPA, FLORIDA
23Y

• • • • • • • • •

I HAVE HAD GLIMPSES OF THE WAY IT'S GOING TO BE with the kids gone—it's quiet, it's calm, there's not a mountain of dirty laundry to clean.

—*CLAUDIA SHAMP*
ATHENS, GEORGIA
21Y

WHEN PEOPLE GET OLDER AND THEIR KIDS MOVE OUT, there's less and less a couple has in common. Make an effort to do things together again. My husband and I both like sports and golf is something men and women can do together. We started practicing together and now play together during the week, which is great.

>   —*HELEN*
>   *MORTON GROVE, ILLINOIS*
>   *40Y*

* * * * * * * *

HAVING AN EMPTY NEST WAS A GREAT CHANGE. It was a freeing experience, not having to worry about where they were and what they were doing. You still worry, but it's not as bad when they live somewhere else. When they are home, you have to wait up until the middle of the night for them to roll in from being out with friends. Suddenly, we could take vacations whenever we wanted and take spur-of-the-moment day trips. The freedom to do things whenever you feel like it is balanced against missing them.

>   —*H.E.R.*
>   *AVERILL PARK, NEW YORK*
>   *44Y*

* * * * * * * *

MY DAUGHTER WAS IN HER FIRST YEAR OF COLLEGE when we moved to Dayton, Ohio with our youngest and left our middle child with a relative to finish his senior year of high school. We went from three kids to one all at once. Suddenly, there is a big empty box. It's shocking, even though you know it's going to happen. You just have to enjoy it as a different phase of your life. You're back as a couple again.

>   —*DOLORES F. JOHNSON*
>   *WICHITA, KANSAS*
>   *55Y*

WE FIND ONE GREAT WAY TO CONNECT is to fantasize and dream about the future together. For the first three years we were married, it was about finding another place to live. Now, 22 years later, we talk about retiring to Mexico. It helps us to stay focused on our future together.

—*B.L.*
KIRKLAND, WASHINGTON
22Y

. . . .

" We work hard to keep it fresh and exciting. We make sure to keep dating even though we have been married for many years. We both are childish and silly and it keeps us happy to be together. I see too many folks acting way too serious. Marriage is to be enjoyed, not endured. "

—*LEE*
PASSAIC, NEW JERSEY

I MET WITH THE MOST UNEXPECTED situation while I was married. I learned something that I never believed as a child: marriage is hard work! Every day—trying to stay connected, to understand each other, communicate and maintain balance in the relationship—is a constant struggle. My then-husband and I were simply not prepared for these challenges. The difficult times and hardships can wreak havoc on even the most sane and balanced person! Having a good marriage requires a constant commitment and reaffirmation to the relationship. Many people can do it. I could not. Yes, the joys of marriage are plentiful if you can keep weathering the storms—and there can be many storms, hurricanes, and typhoons. And rainbows and sunny days. Keep the storms in perspective.

—MELLANESE
WAIKOLOA, HAWAII
34Y,

• • • • • • • • •

WHEN TIMES ARE GOOD, MARRIAGE IS GREAT, but it's the tough times that really test you. In our marriage my husband and I have dealt with some real trials. I survived a brain tumor in my 20s, my husband had a severe heart attack in his 30s, and our son had serious medical problems at birth. My husband took care of our whole family while I was sick, and in a way I was grateful for the chance to do the same for him when he was sick. What I learned from all of this is that the good times are great, but it's the trials that pull you together. I think when you're going through a storm, it may bring you comfort to keep in mind that if you are able to weather it, you'll be a stronger couple when it ends.

—CRYSTAL SMITH
DUBOIS, PENNSYLVANIA
22Y

"Men have a much better time of it than women. For one thing, they marry later; for another thing, they die earlier."

—H.L. MENCKEN

ALWAYS PUT YOUR MARRIAGE BEFORE anything else—your kids, your job, whatever. Our focus was our children. We went to every basketball game, track meet, or Boy Scout event, but we didn't put the same time and attention into each other. When my youngest moved out of the house, we no longer knew how to relate to each other.

—*JOHN*
GREELEY, COLORADO
24Y

• • • • • • • •

THERE'S ONE DISTINCT DIFFERENCE between couples who stay married and couples who get divorced. The difference: Couples who stay married don't get divorced.

—*JIM*
KNOXVILLE, TENNESSEE
19Y

• • • • • • • •

AFTER 35 YEARS OF MARRIAGE, we're off to New Zealand next month for a 3-week honeymoon. Although my wife is a travel agent, we prefer to travel spontaneously—we arrive at our destination, rent a car and find our way through the city or country.

—*ARMANDO DIAZ*
BURLINGAME, CALIFORNIA
35Y

More Wisdom: Good Stuff That Doesn't Fit Anywhere Else

E*very marriage is unique. Sometimes, our experiences defy categorization. For that reason, we present a collection of advice that runs the gamut, from special occasions and big moments in life to the everyday routines of running the house together. Enjoy the advice, and enjoy your marriage while you're at it.*

ON THEIR 50TH WEDDING ANNIVERSARY, I asked my parents the key to their success in marriage. My mother replied: "For the first 30 years, I worked days and Pop worked nights."

—*JOSEPH ORLOVSKY*
MANALAPAN, NEW JERSEY
💔*33Y*

HANG ON! IT'S A WILD RIDE!

—*BOB*
ATLANTA, GEORGIA
💔*14Y*

IF YOU LIKE ACTIVE THINGS, try simple outdoor activities you can do together, like fishing or camping. You don't have to "rough it" or make it difficult. We enjoy fishing together. Last weekend, we anchored down and dropped some lines, and my wife actually touched a fish for the first time and tried to take it off her pole. But it moved, and she dropped it on the deck. I still have to bait her hook with worms—but she's progressing.

—*GREG JANTZ*
PONCA CITY, OKLAHOMA
❤ 7Y

• • • • • • • •

YOU WILL SHARE NO CLOSER MOMENT as husband and wife than when your first child is born. I highly suggest all men take the opportunity to go into the birthing suite or delivery room to share that magic moment. You will not believe what a bonding experience it is between you and your spouse. When you look into each other's eyes right after that baby appears . . . it's like nothing else you will ever experience.

—*MARTIN SEABECK*
FOMBELL, PENNSYLVANIA
❤ 7Y

• • • • • • • •

I REMEMBER WHEN MY BROTHER and I planned our parents' 25th anniversary party, which was a surprise party. It was so much work and cost so much money. It was probably the biggest project I'd ever done. But when they walked into the hall . . . the look on their faces was priceless. I started crying even before my mom did, and that wasn't long. I think that's the night I'll think of when they're gone. You could just see how much in love they still were.

—*TINIKA GILL*
HYATTSVILLE, MARYLAND
NOT MARRIED

HAVING A SENSE OF HUMOR has a lot to do with having success in marriage. If you can't have fun, it won't work.

—JANE
BROOKLYN, NEW YORK
20Y

• • • • • • • •

" Look at your wedding pictures and video periodically to refresh your memory of why you married this person! "

—ANONYMOUS
WASHINGTON, DC
33Y

• • • • • • • •

MARRIAGE IS EASY. We're crazy about each other, we respect each other, we like each other, we have fun together. It's comforting to be with somebody. I come home and complain about my job; she comes home and complains about her job. Once in a while you get on each other's nerves, but so what? It's easy.

—ANONYMOUS
PITTSBURGH, PENNSYLVANIA
8Y

• • • • • • • •

TREAT THE OTHER PERSON AS YOU WOULD a rare violin. Marriage is much more than the wedding day. It takes incredible character and courage to make a lifelong commitment to another human being and to stick with it.

—C.L.
PETALUMA, CALIFORNIA
33Y

LEARN FROM EACH OTHER

Being with my spouse has shown me both the best and worst parts of myself. I can be selfish and bossy, and I can be a giving, creative, cool woman. Interacting with him has opened my eyes to the things I do to limit myself. I have a tendency to be a shy homebody when I don't feel good about myself, and that makes me feel even worse. He doesn't tend to let me stay in that low place very long. Also, my husband has a vast creative vision, whereas mine is more narrow and focused. I didn't realize this about myself before I was married. We balance each other. I can see more possibilities for myself when I'm with him. Also, in past relationships, I feared abandonment, and he got this right away. Being with him taught me that you can fight and have some difficult times without losing the relationship. In fact, struggles can make the relationship stronger. I never knew that until I was married. I guess marriage gives me the security to be angry with him sometimes because I know he's not going to walk away.

—*R.*
AUSTIN, TEXAS
♥ 3Y

BE WILLING TO COMPROMISE. My wife isn't a dog person but I grew up with big dogs in my home and love them. We'd been dating 8 years and then got married and she was finally willing to try having a dog. We both did some research and because she thinks a big dog will eat her, we're going to get a small one.

> —M.A.
> *IOWA CITY, IOWA*
> 2Y

Love who she is, not who she could be, and always try to smell good.

—B.P.
ORLANDO, FLORIDA
3Y

MY FRIENDS AND I STARTED a new tradition two years ago. On the first Saturday of every month, we get together and either go out to dinner or cook together. When cooking, we rotate houses and everybody brings something, whether it's alcohol, a dessert or a side dish. Now that we're starting to have kids, this is a great way to keep in touch.

> —CANDICE PORTER
> *OVERLAND PARK, KANSAS*
> 1Y

I'M A TRUCK DRIVER SO I'M AWAY ON THE ROAD a good portion of the time. I think that's what's kept us together. Absence makes the heart grow fonder. I think there's something to be said for that.

> —JOHN S.
> *EAST PALESTINE, OHIO*
> 18Y

I MADE THE CARDINAL MISTAKE: I thought he would change! Never assume this.

> —L.N.
> *PEAR RIVER, NEW YORK*
> 3Y

"Both men and women live longer, happier, healthier and wealthier lives when they are married." The lifestyle apparently helps men physically, and it helps women financially.

—*National Marriage Project, Rutgers University*

WITH MARRIAGE, EVERYTHING COMES DOWN to one thing—"shlepping stuff from place to place." Suddenly you look back and realize that your life is really about hauling stuff around. Kids, strollers, groceries, etc. all need to be picked up and moved from place to place and this will consume most of your time. I advise you to get a comfortable vehicle.

—*Anonymous*
Brockton, Massachusetts
4Y

• • • • • • • •

THE THING I WONDER ABOUT PEOPLE who aren't married is: What do they do with big decisions? Who do they bounce their ideas off of?

—*C.S.*
San Francisco, California
3Y

• • • • • • • •

I NEED HIM TO JUST LISTEN. When he doesn't listen to what's going on in my life, that really depresses me. Guys don't ever talk about their problems or talk about their days. For girls, it's our way of releasing the tension. Finding the middle ground helps.

—*Barbara*
Puebla, Mexico
9M

• • • • • • • •

ACKNOWLEDGING THE LITTLE THINGS is very important; so is honesty tempered by tact and regard for the other's feelings; but most of all, a person needs to be respected by their mate as an individual. If these traits are not present in a marriage, then the tendency is to seek them elsewhere.

—*R.A.*
Cedar Rapids, Iowa
25Y

MARRIAGE IS NOT EASY. That's just a fact. It is a daily challenge for both of us, but just make sure you are happier more often than you are sad.

—*KRISTIN*
SEATTLE, WASHINGTON
5Y

. . . .

THE BEST POSSIBLE ADVICE I can offer to someone getting married is to take great pleasure in the presence of your spouse. When you ache for the sight of your spouse, the sound of her voice, the touch of her hand, you are in a good place and ready to spend your life with that person. When you are hesitant to reach out for her hand, then you aren't ready. You might get there, or you might not, but it'll work out the best when you want that hand cradled in yours.

—*M.J. TWETTEN*
CHICAGO, ILLINOIS
2Y, 9M

. . . .

ONE OF THE MOST IMPORTANT THINGS when you look for a partner is to find someone who's happy with himself, because if he's not, you'll never be able to make him happy in a marriage. What you see is what you get. You might be able to change the kind of glasses or clothes he wears but you'll never be able to change the kind of person he is.

—*CATHY RAFF*
MACCABIM, ISRAEL
13Y

. . . .

SMALL GESTURES GO A LONG WAY. You don't always have to buy big gifts or make huge declarations to show you care. The small stuff can be more touching.

—*JESSE*
SAN FRANCISCO, CALIFORNIA
5M

FOR THE MEN . . .

REMEMBER HOW MANY TIMES YOUR MOM cleaned your room, or how often she worked to put a meal on the table for you and your family? Do you remember how many times you thanked her? I didn't think so. Well that just isn't going to cut it in your marriage. Your wife is definitely going to work harder than you to keep your home life together, whether she is home full time or working as well; so thank her. Realize how much she does for you, how important it is, and just say thanks.

> —*ANONYMOUS*
> *MINNEAPOLIS, MINNESOTA*
> 💔 5Y

· · · · · · · · ·

YOU PROBABLY SHOULDN'T GO OUT TO ANY STRIP CLUBS after you're married—even if you tell her you went somewhere else.

> —*RICK*
> *ATLANTA, GEORGIA*
> 💔 1Y

· · · · · · · · ·

EVERY YEAR, THE POLICE SKI RACES ARE HELD IN VAIL, and every year, I go. About 10 years ago, however, a week before the races were scheduled to begin, I found out my wife had been nominated for Employee of the Year, and, like a stupid, selfish idiot, I decided to go skiing instead of to her presentation ceremony because I'd already paid for the trip and it was a tradition. She wasn't happy, and although she's only brought it up once since then, I regret that decision to this day, because the internal guilt I've experienced has been far worse. My actions sent the message that the ski races were more important to me than her, which isn't true. If I could do one thing over in our marriage, that would be it.

> —*JOHN COOKE*
> *GREELEY, COLORADO*
> 💔 24Y

SPEAKING MOSTLY TO MEN HERE, resist the temptation to start a serious flirtation or have an affair. Instead, look directly in front of you. There may well be more there than you realize. If something is wrong, it may have to do with your own emotional issues. Confront them in therapy or with whatever vehicle works. An enduring marriage requires that each person feel confident and comfortable with himself/herself.

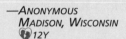

> —*ANONYMOUS*
> *MADISON, WISCONSIN*
> 💔 *12Y*

PICK UP AFTER YOURSELF. Wipe down the counter after you're done shaving. Put your towel on the hook instead of the floor. The little things help.

> —*TINA M. COY*
> *EL CAJON, CALIFORNIA*
> 💔 *25Y*

WOMEN REMEMBER EVERYTHING, and they always know when you're lying.

> —*RICHARD HALL*
> *KENNESAW, GEORGIA*
> 💔 *10Y*

A marriage is all about the wife. A happy wife is a happy home.

—*M.S.*
Minneapolis, Minnesota
6Y

WHAT YOU ARE INITIALLY ATTRACTED TO in someone can be the exact same thing that ultimately drives you crazy. My husband is stable, reliable, and predictable—which completely sold me while we were dating and first married. I still appreciate those qualities, but I often find myself wondering, "Where's his spontaneity? Where's the excitement?" You can't have it both ways. Just be careful that you really do want what you think you want—forever.

—*R.*
Denver, Colorado

• • • • • • • •

ROMANTIC PROPOSAL DINNER: $105
Simple wedding gown: $350
Five-day honeymoon in Walt Disney World: $2,500
Having a husband who brings you a blanket when you're cold, makes you chicken soup when you're sick, and can fix anything that's broken: Priceless.

—*Jennifer Bright Reich*
Hellertown, Pennsylvania
1Y

• • • • • • • •

MARRIAGES ARE SO UNIQUE—what works for one couple doesn't necessarily apply to the next. There was this man who came to fix my computer; 6 months later, we got married because he needed to get a work visa. There aren't too many people who could meet under our circumstances and still be married 13 years later, but it's worked really well for us. We get along really great, he makes me laugh, we have a ton of fun together. Take all advice with a grain of salt, and don't compare your relationship to others!

—*Anna London*
Melbourne, Australia
13Y

I LIKE SHARING MY LIFE WITH MY WIFE, and sharing her experiences, sharing the little pleasures of life. I like being able to approach life as a team and share the burdens. I enjoy the intimacies of life with a woman, sharing a bed and, of course, sex. When you can share each other's lives and support each other and do that with love and respect for each other, life is better.

—*ANONYMOUS*
LOS ANGELES, CALIFORNIA
11Y

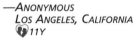 A couple that canoes together stays together. Be sure to keep canoeing!

—*JIM*
ATLANTA, GEORGIA
26Y

FOR US, TRUST WAS ALWAYS THE KEY. Before you marry, do your homework in this area. Test him in many different situations and then you will make sure when you are married, your trust in him will be perfect and can be built upon. In marriage, you need to KNOW he is rock solid.

—*ANONYMOUS*
MONTCLAIR, NEW JERSEY

ALWAYS LET WOMEN MAKE AS MANY suggestions as possible. That way they think they are letting you make the decision based on their suggestions (even though you've already decided!).

—*J.P.*
DAVENPORT, IOWA
30Y

FOR THE LADIES . . .

LADIES, REMEMBER THAT YOU ARE WIVES FIRST. Don't neglect your husbands. We can spend all our energy thinking about our children's summer plans, their homework, their friends, etc. But, we need to consider our husband's needs. It takes effort to make your husband feel loved and respected. If he's happy, it'll be better for the whole family. If you think you can just focus on your kids and neglect your husband because he's a grown man who can fend for himself, you run the risk that someone else will step in and make him feel special. That's a reality.

> —*ANONYMOUS*
> *LIVERPOOL, NEW YORK*
> 💔*10Y*

* * * * * * * * *

DON'T TELL HIM EVERYTHING ABOUT YOUR GIRLFRIENDS (and social life). Whenever you're pissed off or fighting he may use some of it against you.

> —*E.L.*
> *RENO, NEVADA*
> 💔*3Y*

* * * * * * * * *

KNOW GOING INTO YOUR MARRIAGE whether or not your husband is "handy." My husband barely knows which end of a hammer to use to pound nails. I remember one Christmas when I had to buy a saw so I could cut the bottom off of our Christmas tree. I knew if I asked my husband to do it he'd end up cutting his fingers off.

> —*JILL FULLEN*
> *PITTSBURGH, PENNSYLVANIA*
> 💔*31Y*

SOMEONE ONCE SAID THAT THE BIGGEST MISTAKE people make is buying into the myth that their spouse is supposed to be their best friend. This doesn't work because men and women think very differently. For that reason, I joined a women's sorority that meets two times per month. It's my time to be a silly girl again—we talk about our husbands all night long, which is tremendous fun and a great outlet. To get your emotional needs met, you need people you can share things with who understand who you are and how you're wired. Same-sex relationships help keep a balance in yourself, which makes you a better spouse.

> —KARA JOHNSTON
> KLAMATH FALLS, OREGON
> 💔11Y

LOOK IN THE MIRROR EVERY 10 YEARS. Don't think you can gain 75 pounds and your spouse will still think you look great. If you're a size 10 when you get married, stay that way. Have pride in how you look.

> —GUADALUPE GOMEZ
> AZUSA, CALIFORNIA
> 💔37Y

ROAD TRIPS AREN'T RELAXING FOR US. We always argue because he tailgates. How do I deal with it? Make sure we fly.

—*RENAE*
ATLANTA, GEORGIA
3Y

. . . .

"**When you go to a wedding with your wife, don't be embarrassed to get up and dance with her. For most people it's the only time they ever go dancing anymore. Usually you just see the men slow dancing and then they vacate the floor when the faster music starts, leaving the women out there to dance alone. Don't be afraid to show them your moves! You might just get lucky when you get home.**"

—*MARTY L.*
EAST LIVERPOOL, OHIO
15Y

. . . .

KEEP MAKING SUGGESTIONS. When men come up with an idea, they think it's their own!

—*S.P.*
DAVENPORT, IOWA
30Y

I THINK A LOT OF PEOPLE GIVE UP too easily and approach marriage from a selfish perspective. Don't think so much about yourself. Think about the other person. Always put the other person first and try not to hurt their feelings. Love them a lot and tell them so.

—*NORA HAMMOND*
LOUISVILLE, KENTUCKY
50Y

Marry tall and handsome.

—*ADAIR MORELAND*
KEARNY,
NEW JERSEY
45Y

• • • • • • • •

MY WIFE AND I HAVE NO KIDS but two Golden Retrievers. Pets are your marriage's best friend because all they want is unconditional love and they never talk back.

—*JIM MCADAM*
PRESQUE ISLE, WISCONSIN
16Y

• • • • • • • •

I WAS OFTEN CONFUSED BETWEEN love and something else. Make sure it is real love before your marriage begins. Never marry out of desperation. You will divorce the same way.

—*LUBA FURTAK*
CLIFTON

• • • • • • • •

INSTEAD OF BEING A TV SPORTS JUNKIE, try to get out and get active and include your wife when you can. My wife can give me a run for my money on the tennis courts, and even though she can't keep up with me on a bike if I'm going full tilt, we still have a great time biking together on days when I just want an easier ride. It's good for the waistline *and* the marriage.

—*SAM*
SANTA MONICA, CALIFORNIA
14Y

HAPPY ANNIVERSARIES

WE USUALLY HAVE A QUIET ANNIVERSARY—just dinner away from the children is enough. My husband has a hard time remembering the anniversary date. One year, he brought flowers the week before.

—PATRICIA
BROOKLYN, NEW YORK
16Y

USE THE OPPORTUNITY TO MEANINGFULLY REMIND your wife why you married her in the first place. Write it down, or record a video message. But put it in your own words. And take the day off.

—DAN DUPONT
ARLINGTON, VIRGINIA
7Y

FOR OUR 15TH ANNIVERSARY, we went back to Paris, where we'd had our honeymoon. Of course, we did lots of different things this time, since we were at a different stage in life, but we also had a lot of fun going down memory lane and trying to find that cute little bistro or bakery we remembered. It was a great way to remember that exciting feeling of being a newlywed.

—HEIDI
CHICAGO, ILLINOIS
17Y

I CALLED A FEW RESTAURANTS THAT HAD SPECIAL MEMORIES for us and convinced them to give me the recipe for some specific dish there. I asked for easy-ish ones that I could make at home. About a week before our first anniversary, I made a special surprise candlelit dinner of these dishes. It was one of the most wonderful evenings, and years later my husband still raves about that meal.

—N. CLARK
HOUSTON TEXAS
4Y

RECENTLY, OUR TRADITION HAS BEEN TO SHARE a pound of shrimp cocktail, lobster tails and a bottle of champagne at home after the children are in bed. Come to think of it, that's how we celebrate New Year's Eve, too, so I guess we've found a ritual that really works for us.

—*DARCY*
RIVERSIDE, ILLINOIS
❤️ *14Y*

• • • • • • • • •

THE LONGER YOU'VE BEEN MARRIED the more important it is to go all out when you are celebrating anniversaries. Don't skimp. Party hard. My wife and I go to the same restaurant every year but we never order the same meal. And afterward we go to the same spot that I took her on our first date and we just talk. We talk about the year that just passed and what we expect of the year to come.

—*STEVE O'HODNICK*
SWISSVALE, PENNSYLVANIA
❤️ *9Y*

• • • • • • • • •

MY HUBBY AND I ALWAYS CELEBRATE EACH ANNIVERSARY by buying something for the house. For our first anniversary, we bought a lovely mantel clock that sits above our fireplace, chiming away, to this day. Everyone remembers when we got it, and we count the age of the clock with the age of our marriage. Our kids know it was our anniversary present to each other, and I think (I hope) it's a reminder to them that their parents love one another very much, and that our marriage has stood the test of time.

—*ANONYMOUS*
DENVER, COLORADO
❤️ *22Y*

ONE OF THE MOST SPECIAL TIMES to be married is during Christmas. If you are lucky enough to be married during Christmas do something special. Create special traditions that you and your spouse can look forward to year after year. My wife and I always spend Christmas Eve alone no matter how many party invitations we get.

> —DAN SANTOS
> GREEN TREE, PENNSYLVANIA
> 💕 6Y

• • • • • • • •

REPEAT THE STORY OF YOUR WEDDING every year— its beauty, its humorous parts and those areas of special meaning.

> —ANONYMOUS
> PORTLAND, MAINE
> 💕 15Y

• • • • • • • •

WE DECIDED TO GIVE EACH OTHER small gifts on our anniversary, based on the traditional gift list. Year one is paper, so my wife gave me a book she thought I'd like with a touching inscription, and I gave her a love letter. Year two is cotton. My wife got me a beautiful sweater that matches my eyes, and I got her sexy underwear (cotton, not silk, of course). We can't wait for year three: leather!

> —M.F.
> SAN FRANCISCO, CALIFORNIA
> 💕 2Y

• • • • • • • •

THE LAW OF AVERAGES STATES that if you give in and accept your spouse's point of view some- times, there's eventually going to be a balance in the number of times they do the same for you.

> —JOE HOLLIMAN
> CENTENNIAL, COLORADO
> 💕 33Y

TAKE AS MANY PHOTOS of all the important events in your marriage that you can afford. And then take some that you can't afford. When you look back on that stuff later the price you paid for the film is going to seem very insignificant. Get a good camera and snap away.

—*PAULA GRUBBS*
RENFREW, PENNSYLVANIA
💔*13Y*

• • • • • • • •

THREE SIMPLE WORDS: Communicate, Compromise, Compassion.

—*NOLA SMITH*
TAMPA, FLORIDA
💔*23Y*

• • • • • • • •

WHEN I HAVE SOMETHING GOOD TO EAT, I often ask my husband, "Do you want a bite?" thinking that he'll really take just one bite. He never says no and his idea of a bite is to eat the whole darn thing. Then, if I'm lucky, I am left with the crumbs. This always seems to happen when I'm the hungriest. But no matter how often he does this, I never learn. I still let him bite everything. Why? I love him.

—*LEAH LUBIN*
CLEVELAND, OHIO
💔*1Y*

• • • • • • • •

LEARN TO SAY, "YES, DEAR" QUICKLY. When you are in an argument, you are wrong even when you think you are right.

—*HUGH GRAN*
NEW YORK, NEW YORK

"May the gods grant you all things which your heart desires, and may they give you a husband and a home and gracious concord, for there is nothing greater and better than this— when a husband and wife keep a household in oneness of mind, a great woe to their enemies and joy to their friends, and in high renown."

—*HOMER*

GOT RELIGION?

MOST IMPORTANT CHARACTERISTIC FOR A GOOD MARRIAGE PARTNER: same religion or spiritual beliefs. My husband and I are Jewish. I didn't go looking for a Jewish man to marry and my parents didn't require it of me. But when we met, we just knew that we were right for each other, and having the same religion made our bond even stronger. Marriage is tough enough without having to argue over religion or spiritual beliefs.

—*E.G.*
NEW HAVEN, CONNECTICUT
💔*27Y*

• • • • • • • •

THERE'S NO GREATER FEELING than having your spouse sitting with you at church. I went a year without him. Now it's been about a year with him. At first, he didn't want to go. I knew I wasn't going to be able to change his mind, and didn't want to be too pushy. I had to let him go at his own pace. We had a barbecue and invited everyone from church. He liked the people. He started coming. It was a bonding experience. Now, we have the same standards.

—*D.D.*
BRIDGEPORT, NEW YORK
💔*3Y*

• • • • • • • •

WHEN I MET MY SPOUSE, she was a practicing Christian. I'm an atheist, but I've always respected her religious beliefs. She respected mine, and thus it was never an issue. We both believed that religion was a personal thing, and people had to find the path that worked for them. If we went to her family's house for dinner, I would bow my head while her father would give prayer before a meal. It wasn't that I was praying, but rather respecting his family's religious beliefs.

—*JOHN RODGERS*
SEATTLE, WASHINGTON
💔*10Y*

I WOULD NEVER MARRY SOMEONE who didn't put God first. Having similar beliefs has helped us learn together. When I don't understand something I read in the Bible, I ask my husband. Then, we talk about it. Praying together, which we do, clues us into what the other is thinking. It would be 100 times more difficult if we didn't share the same religious beliefs.

—*TERI BURNS*
SYRACUSE, NEW YORK
2M

· · · · · · · · ·

WE SHARE THE SAME VIEWS and it has helped us a lot. If nothing else, it gives us something to discuss. We're Buddhist and, often, aspects of the Dharma are left to interpretation, so we discuss it and usually come to a mutual conclusion. When we do disagree, it's usually a matter of "that's who you are" and we let it go.

—*STACI PRIEST*
PFLUGERVILLE, TEXAS
6Y

· · · · · · · · ·

WE WERE BOTH ATHEISTS. I think if either of us had had strong religious faith, we would never have gotten married in the first place.

—*K.M.*
STANFORD, CALIFORNIA
18Y

· · · · · · · · ·

I THINK IT'S IMPORTANT TO HAVE A RELIGIOUS TRADITION that you can pass on to your children so that they can feel proud of themselves, so that they feel like they belong to a larger group, and so that they have a community of supportive people they feel they can turn to in times of need.

—*L.B.*
CINCINNATI, OHIO
35Y

A FEW WORDS OF WISDOM FOR THE LADIES:
1) When you're home, be informal. You don't have to look good or act feminine all the time. You have to feel at home at home! 2) Sex shifts from crazy to occasional. You haven't lost your appeal; it's a normal part of a busy married life. 3) Talk to your friends before you talk to your parents about issues. 4) Expect to see patterns of your parents. 5) Pick your battles. 6) If you know there's something about yourself that you don't like (something that makes you feel guilty), you need to ask your partner to not allow you to get away with it!

—*DANIELLE*
TORONTO, ONTARIO, CANADA
5M (WITH PARTNER FOR 10 YEARS)

• • • • • • • •

"In marriage you are part of the same team, so don't keep score."

—*JANIS BLAISE*
DIABLO, CALIFORNIA
31Y

• • • • • • • •

ALL YOU HUSBANDS OUT THERE, TAKE NOTE:
Women don't need tons of diamond bracelets. Not that some women would complain, mind you. But don't think you need to spend money constantly to keep romance in the marriage. A small bouquet of flowers or—even less expensive, a sweet handwritten note—will do that just fine. That's what we really want!

—*RACHEL B.*
PHILADELPHIA, PENNSYLVANIA
7Y

GOOD ADVICE FOR MEN ONLY: When she wants to talk, turn off the TV. Good advice for women only: If he's watching TV, it's probably not a good time to talk.

—*JILLIAN LEWIS*
BROOKLYN, NEW YORK
18M

● ● ● ● ● ● ● ●

ARM YOURSELF WITH INFORMATION if you're having a problem. I have troubles with PMS. Two days out of the month I am not myself. Honestly, I should come with a warning label. Things that normally wouldn't bother me a bit make me furious, and my husband is the biggest target. In total frustration, I went to a counselor about it. She told me that when women are at a certain point in their menstrual cycles, it's like a filter is removed. Words or actions that normally would just bounce off because of that protective filter get through like pointy arrows. This was one of the biggest "aha" moments in my life. I explained this to my husband, so he knows to tread a bit more lightly those days.

—*ANONYMOUS*
HELLERTOWN, PENNSYLVANIA
1Y

● ● ● ● ● ● ● ●

IT TOOK ME YEARS TO LEARN HOW to let my wife complain about something without me trying to offer solutions. A lot of times she just wants me to hug and comfort her or agree with her about how awful the situation is. If I don't know whether I'm supposed to console or help come up with solutions, I just ask outright.

—*SEAN H.*
NEW YORK, NEW YORK
15Y

TOP TEN QUESTIONS YOU SHOULD NEVER ASK YOUR HUSBAND

1. DOES THIS SKIRT MAKE ME LOOK FAT? Of course he will answer no (unless he is a complete idiot). But, if he loves you, he does not care if you look fat in that skirt. You should love him enough not to ask such a loaded question.

2. WHAT ARE YOU THINKING? Men are not complicated. If he is thinking about something he wants to share, he will tell you.

3. DO YOU THINK THAT GIRL IS PRETTY? Most likely, the answer is yes, she's pretty. But if you love your husband, don't put him on the spot just because you're feeling insecure.

4. DO THESE SHOES GO WITH THIS DRESS? There is no way your husband can answer that question. Men have two pairs of shoes for casual or dress attire. How would he know?

5. WOULD YOU LIKE TO GO TO THE BALLET THIS FRIDAY NIGHT? With few exceptions, the answer is NO. This also goes for the symphony, poetry readings and that upcoming women's songwriter festival.

6. CAN YOU RUN TO THE STORE AND GRAB ME SOME TAMPONS? If you hate your husband enough to ask this question, it might be time to find a divorce lawyer.

7. HOW DO YOU LIKE MY NEW HAIRCUT? He'll likely answer, "Did you get your hair cut?" Unless you've had a foot of hair removed, he won't know the difference. Besides, he loves you, not your hair, so why ask?

8. DOES MY MAKEUP LOOK OK? Let's face it. Women dress and put on make-up for other women to notice them, not our husbands.

9. WHICH SHADE OF YELLOW DO YOU THINK WILL GO WITH THE WALLPAPER IN THE KITCHEN? They all look yellow to him. It doesn't matter if it is dandelion yellow or a lemon-beige.

10. CAN YOU HOLD MY PURSE WHILE I'M IN THE DRESSING ROOM? If your husband answers yes to this question, then you have successfully removed his manhood. Congratulations, you're no longer married to a man.

—*VIRGINIA ROBERSON*
FRANKLIN, TENNESSEE
💔 *12Y*

TRADITIONAL
WEDDING
ANNIVERSARY
GIFTS:
1st Year: Paper
10th Year: Tin,
Aluminum
15th Year:
Crystal
25th Year:
Silver
50th Year:
Gold
75th Year:
Diamond

ONCE I GOT OLD ENOUGH TO APPRECIATE that my husband was a full-blown adult human who had chosen of his own free will to try to live alongside me—and not someone whose sole purpose in life was to be changed by me—I found him fascinating. Still do. He's very intelligent, kind and hard working in all things. That makes him interesting. We try to mine our interests a lot and try to make time to really talk to one another.

—MARION ROACH SMITH
TROY, NEW YORK
15Y

• • • • • • • •

MY WIFE AND I HAVE A LOT of the same interests. We both love the Allman Brothers Band, "Airplane!" and Mexican food. (Yeah, I know how good I've got it.) But even so, she has some "girlie" habits that I want no part of. I can't understand how she can talk to the same friend *twice* in the same week, let alone in the same day, and what the appeal of "The Bachelor" is. I assume she feels the same way the few times I invite my friends over to do endless shots of Wild Turkey while watching the DVD of "Escape From New York." When that happens, it's more than acceptable to give your spouse some space. You don't have to share all your interests or even always be able to tolerate them. Remember that it's a sign of a good relationship that you can still do your own thing once in a while.

—ROSS WARNER
NEW YORK, NEW YORK
1Y

• • • • • • • •

MARRIAGE IS A ROLLER COASTER RIDE. If you don't get off on the bottom, eventually you'll rise up again to the top.

—TERRI SKALABRIN
SEATTLE, WASHINGTON
13Y

DON'T DISCUSS MONEY or old lovers in bed.

—*HUGH FOLEY*
STILLWATER, OKLAHOMA
💔 *10Y*

• • • • • • • •

MARRIAGE IS LIKE INVESTING in the stock market. Commit to your investment and don't sell out! Remember, there will be cycles of despairing lows and dizzying heights. If you hold on long enough, you'll have a rich life. Then people will be asking YOU for advice.

—*KATHY*
LAUREL, MARYLAND
💔 *33Y*

• • • • • • • •

NO ONE SAYS MARRIAGE IS EASY. Especially the Lifers. I am going on 30 years of marriage, and can tell you there were times when I wondered where the map was. The answer is: There is no map. Use your instincts. And remember your partner feels just the same. Being with someone is very comforting for many reasons—not the least of which is that humans are companionable creatures. If you've found someone with whom you can yell, smile, snore, belch, rage, relax, talk or just be silent, then you are a survivor.

—*CHRISTINE EMMERT*
VALLEY FORGE, PENNSYLVANIA
💔 *30Y*

SPECIAL THANKS

Thanks to our intrepid "headhunters" for going out to find so many married folks from around the country with interesting advice to share:

Jamie Allen, Chief Headhunter

Jennifer Blaise	R.M. Lofton	Jennifer Bright Reich
Scott Deckman	Ken McCarthy	Dana Rothblatt
Elizabeth Edwardsen	Lindsey Roth Miller	Beth Turney Rutchik
Sara Faiwell	Jennifer Nittoso	Graciela Sholander
Shannon Hurd	Christina Orlovsky	Laura Roe Stevens
Teena Hammond	Adam Pollock	Jade Walker
Lisa Jaffe Hubbell	Peter Ramirez	Sara Walker
Natasha Lambropoulos	William Ramsey	Wendy Webb
Nicole Lessin	Kazz Regelman	Jennifer Weiner

Thanks, too, to our editorial advisor Alys R. Yablon. And thanks to our assistant, Miri Greidi, for her yeoman's work at keeping us all organized.

The real credit for this book, of course, goes to all the people whose experiences and collective wisdom make up this guide. There are too many of you to thank individually, of course, but you know who you are. Thanks for sharing.

CREDITS

Page 8: *Cosmopolitan Magazine*, October 2004

Page 10: Bob Nachshin is the author of *I Do, You Do . . . But Just Sign Here: A Quick and Easy Guide to Cohab, Prenup and Postnup Agreements*

Page 12: *Seattle Times*, May 2004

Page 13: *Harvard University Gazette*, October 16, 2003

Page 14: bmj.bmjjournals.com/cgi/content/full/326/7383/277

Page 16: *The Top 10 of Everything*, by Russell Ash, Dorling Kindersley, 2004

Page 19: Guinness Book of World Records, 2004 edition

Page 32: traveltraveltravel.com, 2004 stats

Page 37: Sharon Naylor is a wedding expert and author of 23 wedding books, including *Your Special Wedding Vows*

Page 39: *Journal of Personality and Psychology*, as quoted in *Health Day News* on May 17, 2004

Page 45: CNN, March 17, 2003

Page 47: About.com, "The History of Marriage" http://marriage.about.com/od/historyofmarriage/

Page 51: *Newlywed Debt: The Anti-Dowry*, by James P. Marshall, Ph.D., L.M.F.T. & Linda Skogrand, Ph.D.

Page 54: Zsa Zsa Gabor, Quote DB, http://www.quotedb.com/quotes/1641

Page 57: Girls and Boys Town, December 15, 2003

Page 64: *The Wall Street Journal*, "The Key to a Lasting Marriage: Combat," November 4, 2004

Page 67: Ogden Nash (1902-1971), "To Keep Your Marriage Brimming"

Page 71: *The Wall Street Journal*, "The Key to a Lasting Marriage: Combat," November 4, 2004

Page 74: "The Seven Principles of Making Marriage Work," by John M. Gottman, Ph.D., 1999

Page 78: *Couple Talk: How to Talk Your Way to a Great Relationship*, by Chick Moorman and Thomas Haller, M.Div., M.S.W., A.C.S.W., ©2003, Chick Moorman, Thomas Haller and Personal Power Press

Page 81: www.expage.com/crazykissezstats

Page 89: "Hard Living, Perceived Entitlement to a Great Marriage, and Marital Dissolution" by Sanchez, L., and C.T. Gager, in *Journal of Marriage and Family*, Volume 63 (2000): 708-722

Page 99: *Newlywed Debt: The Anti-Dowry*, by James P. Marshall, Ph.D., L.M.F.T. & Linda Skogrand, Ph.D.

Page 103: "Happily Married With Kids: It's Not Just a Fairy Tale," by Carol Ummel Lindquist, Ph.D., 2004

Page 109: Rodney Dangerfield, Brainy Quote, http://www.brainyquote.com/quotes/quotes/r/rodneydang167277.html

Page 115: "Balancing It All" by Nancy Hoffman, R.N., L.P.C. liferelationships.com

Page 118: Lovegevity.com, "Ten Great Dates to Energize Your Marriage" http://www.lovegevity.com/marriage/expertadvice/tgddr1.html

Page 127: Column in *O Magazine*, October 2004

Page 154: *Why Men Don't Have a Clue and Women Always Need More Shoes: The Ultimate Guide to the Opposite Sex*, by Barbara and Allan Pease, ©2004, Broadway Books

Page 156: "Chores, Chores, Chores" by Sheri and Bob Stritof, www.about.com

Page 167: www.expage.com/crazykissezstats

Page 170: Health Psychology, September 2004

Page 172: Maria Isbell is the President of Kidsncommon.com

Page 191: www.match.com

Page 193: *Christian Science Monitor*, September 15, 2004

Page 199: Associated Press, October 7, 2004

Page 214: *Minneapolis Star Tribune*, September 30, 2004

Page 219: CNN, March 17, 2003

Page 225: H.L. Mencken quote, Quote Garden, http://www.quotegarden.com/marriage.html

Page 232: National Marriage Project, Rutgers University, "The Top 10 Myths About Marriage," 2002

Page 245: Homer, c. 700 B.C.

HELP YOUR FRIENDS SURVIVE!

Order extra copies of *How to Survive Your Marriage.*

Check your local bookstore, www.hundredsofheads.com, or use this form.

Please send me _____ copies of *How to Survive Your Marriage.*

Enclose $13.95 for each copy. Add $3.00 for shipping and handling for one book, and $1.00 for each additional book. Georgia residents must add 4% sales tax. Kansas residents add 5.3% sales tax. Payment must accompany orders. Please allow 3 weeks for delivery.

My check for $_____ is enclosed.
Please charge my __ Visa __ MasterCard __ American Express

Name _____

Organization _____

Address _____

City/State/Zip _____

Phone _____Email _____

Credit card # _____

Exp. Date _____Signature _____

Please make checks payable to HUNDREDS OF HEADS BOOKS, INC.

Please fax to 212-937-2220, or mail to:

HUNDREDS OF HEADS BOOKS, INC.
#230
2221 Peachtree Road, Suite D
Atlanta, Georgia 30309

HELP WRITE THE NEXT Hundreds of Heads™ SURVIVAL GUIDE!

Tell us your story about a life experience, and what lesson you learned from it. If we use your story in one of our books, we'll send you a free copy. Use this card or visit www.hundredsofheads.com.

Here's my story/advice on surviving

❏ **A NEW JOB** (years working:_____ profession/job:_____)

❏ **A MOVE** (# of times you've moved:____) ❏ **A DIET** (# of lbs. lost in best diet: ____)

❏ **A TEENAGER** (ages/sexes of your children: _____)

❏ **DIVORCE** (times married: _____ times divorced:_____)

❏ **MARRIAGE** (years married: _____)

❏ **A BABY** (ages/sexes of your children: _____)

❏ _____ **OTHER TOPIC** (you pick)

Name: _____City/State: _____

❏ Use my name ❏ Use my initials only ❏ Anonymous

(Note: Your entry in the book may also include city/state and the descriptive information above.)

How should we contact you *(this will not be published or shared):*

email: _____ other: _____

Please mail to:

HUNDREDS OF HEADS BOOKS, INC.
2221 Peachtree Road, Suite D-230
Atlanta, Georgia 30309

Your story/advice:

ABOUT THE EDITORS

YADIN KAUFMANN is a founder of a venture capital firm that invests in high-technology start-up companies. He got his B.A. at Princeton, though he spent more time there with his future wife, Lori, than in the library. It paid off—they've survived 22 years together—and counting.

LORI BANOV KAUFMANN is a business consultant, and holds an AB from Princeton University and an M.B.A. from the Harvard Business School. She and Yadin have been married for 22 years; together they have produced four great books and four even more terrific children.

JAMIE ALLEN is an editor and "chief headhunter" for the HUNDREDS OF HEADS™ survival guide series. He has worked as a producer in television news, and he spent five years as a senior writer and editor for CNN.com. He lives in Atlanta with his wife and two children. A nine-year veteran of marriage, Jamie is smartly planning something special for his wife on their 10th anniversary.

VISIT WWW.HUNDREDSOFHEADS.COM

Do you have something interesting to say about marriage, your in-laws, dieting, holding a job, or one of life's other challenges?

 Help humanity—share your story!

 Get published in our next book!

 Find out about the upcoming titles in the HUNDREDS OF HEADS™ survival guide series!

 Read up-to-the-minute advice on many of life's challenges!

 Sign up to become an interviewer for one of the next HUNDREDS OF HEADS™ survival guides!

Visit www.hundredsofheads.com today!

Other Books from HUNDREDS OF HEADS™ BOOKS

HOW TO SURVIVE YOUR FRESHMAN YEAR . . . by Hundreds of Sophomores, Juniors, and Seniors Who Did (and some things to avoid, from a few dropouts who didn't)™
(April 2004; ISBN 0-9746296-0-0)

HOW TO SURVIVE DATING . . . by Hundreds of Happy Singles Who Did (and some things to avoid, from a few broken hearts who didn't)™
(October 2004; ISBN 0-9746296-1-9)

HOW TO SURVIVE YOUR BABY'S FIRST YEAR . . . by Hundreds of Happy Parents Who Did (and some things to avoid, from a few who barely made it)™
(January 2005; ISBN 0-9746296-2-7)

HOW TO SURVIVE YOUR TEENAGER . . . by Hundreds of Still-Sane Parents Who Did (and some things to avoid, from a few whose kids drove them nuts)™
(Spring 2005; ISBN 0-9746296-3-5)

HOW TO SURVIVE A MOVE . . . by Hundreds of Happy People Who Did (and some things to avoid, from a few who haven't upacked yet)™
(Spring 2005; 0-9746292-5-1)

HOW TO SURVIVE YOUR DIVORCE . . . by Hundreds of Happy Exes Who Did (and some things to avoid, from a few who haven't gotten over it yet)™
(Spring 2005; 0-9746292-6-X)

Here's my story/advice on surviving

❑ **DATING**   ❑ **FRESHMAN YEAR** (college and year of graduation: _____)
❑ **MARRIAGE** (years married: _____) ❑ **A NEW JOB** (years working:_____ profession/job: _____)
❑ **YOUR BABY'S FIRST YEAR** (ages/sexes of your children:_____)
❑ **A MOVE** (# of times you've moved:_____) ❑ **DIVORCE** (times married:_____ times divorced:_____)
❑ **DIET** (# of lbs. you've lost in best diet: _____) ❑ _____ **OTHER TOPIC** (you pick)

Name:_____ City/State: _____

❑ Use my name   ❑ Use my initials only   ❑ Anonymous
(Your entry in the book may also include city/state and the descriptive information above.)

How should we contact you *(this will not be published or shared)*:
email: _____ other: _____

Here's my story/advice: _____
_____
_____
_____
_____
_____
_____

need more room? visit www.hundredsofheads.com

HELP WRITE THE NEXT Hundreds of Heads™ SURVIVAL GUIDE!

Tell us your story about a life experience, and what lesson you learned from it.
If we use your story in one of our books, we'll send you a free copy.
Use this card or visit www.hundredsofheads.com (indicate 'referred by BRC').

Here's my story/advice on surviving

❑ **DATING**   ❑ **FRESHMAN YEAR** (college and year of graduation: _____)
❑ **MARRIAGE** (years married: _____) ❑ **A NEW JOB** (years working:_____ profession/job: _____)
❑ **YOUR BABY'S FIRST YEAR** (ages/sexes of your children:_____)
❑ **A MOVE** (# of times you've moved:_____) ❑ **DIVORCE** (times married:_____ times divorced:_____)
❑ **DIET** (# of lbs. you've lost in best diet: _____) ❑ _____ **OTHER TOPIC** (you pick)

Name:_____ City/State: _____

❑ Use my name   ❑ Use my initials only   ❑ Anonymous
(Your entry in the book may also include city/state and the descriptive information above.)

How should we contact you *(this will not be published or shared)*:
email: _____ other: _____

Here's my story/advice: _____
_____
_____
_____
_____
_____
_____

need more room? visit www.hundredsofheads.com

Waiver: All entries are property of Hundreds of Heads Books, Inc., and may be edited, published in any medium, etc. By submitting content, you grant Hundreds of Heads Books, Inc. and its affiliates a royalty-free, perpetual, irrevocable, non-exclusive right (including any moral rights) and license to use, reproduce, modify, adapt, publish, translate, create derivative works from, distribute, communicate to the public, perform and display the content (in whole or in part) worldwide and/or to incorporate it in other works in any form, media, or technology now known or later developed, for the full term of any Rights that may exist in such content, and to identify you (with the information above) as the contributor of content you submit.

Ref. _____

BUSINESS REPLY MAIL

FIRST-CLASS MAIL   PERMIT NO. 220   ATLANTA, GA

POSTAGE WILL BE PAID BY ADDRESSEE

HUNDREDS OF HEADS BOOKS, INC.
#230
2221 Peachtree Road, Suite D
Atlanta, Georgia 30309

NO POSTAGE
NECESSARY
IF MAILED
IN THE
UNITED STATES

BUSINESS REPLY MAIL

FIRST-CLASS MAIL   PERMIT NO. 220   ATLANTA, GA

POSTAGE WILL BE PAID BY ADDRESSEE

HUNDREDS OF HEADS BOOKS, INC.
#230
2221 Peachtree Road, Suite D
Atlanta, Georgia 30309